MW01392365

ANATHEMA!

Plate 1

ANATHEMA!

Medieval Scribes and the History of Book Curses

MARC DROGIN

ALLANHELD & SCHRAM

ALLANHELD, OSMUN & CO. PUBLISHERS, INC.
Totowa, New Jersey

ABNER SCHRAM LTD.
Montclair, New Jersey

Published in the United States of America in 1983
by Allanheld, Osmun & Co (A Division of Littlefield, Adams & Co.),
81 Adams Drive, Totowa, N.J. 07512 and by Abner Schram Ltd.,
36 Park Street, Montclair, N.J. 07042.

Copyright ©1983 by Marc Drogin

All rights reserved. No part of this publication may be
reproduced, stored in a retrieval system, or transmitted
in any form or by any means, electronic, mechanical, photo-
copying, recording, or otherwise, without the prior permission
of the publisher.

83 84 85 / 10 9 8 7 6 5 4 3 2 1

Printed in the United States of America

To Robbie, Annie, Eric and Martha

*   *   *

And to the memory of George Prior, a special friend whose enthusiastic and knowledgeable career in books and publishing enriched the lives of so many others. A part of the pleasure in writing this book was my anticipation of the delight I hoped he would find in it.

May this volume continue in motion
And its pages each day be unfurl'd,
Till an ant has drunk up the ocean,
Or a tortoise has crawl'd round the world.
      Paris, 1507. From W. Roberts' *Book-Verse—*
      An Anthology of Poems of Books and Bookmen
      from the Earliest Times to Recent Years
      (London, 1896)

CONTENTS

Illustrations   ix
Preface   xiii
Acknowledgments   xvii
INTRODUCTION   xix
HOW BOOKS WERE WRITTEN   1
THE CARE OF BOOKS - BESEECHED   17
THE VALUE OF BOOKS   29
THE CARE OF BOOKS - DECREED   36
ANATHEMA   46
Appendix - A CONFUSION OF BOOKS   112
Sources   129
Explicit   138

> *O for a Booke and a shadie nooke,*
> *Eyther in-a-doore or out,*
> *With the greene leaves whisp'ring overhede,*
> *Or the Streete cryes all about,*
> *Where I may Reade all at my ease,*
> *Both of the Newe and Olde,*
> *For a jollie goode Booke, whereon to looke,*
> *Is better to me than Golde.*
>
>   Old English song[76]

ILLUSTRATIONS

Plate		Page
1	SCRIBAL WORK. The 6th-century B.C. philosopher and mathematician Pythagoras, shown at work in a sculpture detail from the exterior of Chartres Cathedral, Chartres, France. (Courtesy of Editions Houvet, Chartres)	ii
2	MEDIEVAL MAN IN ANGUISH. A gargoyle from the exterior of New College, Oxford. Originally carved shortly after 1375, this recent reproduction replaced the original, which had suffered the anguish of time. (Courtesy of New College, Oxford University)	xxii
3	THE LABOR OF BOOK PRODUCTION. Nine vignettes of the 12th century, showing the creation of a book. (Courtesy of the Staatsbibliothek Bamberg, Bamberg, West Germany)	4
4	A MONK'S OWN BOOK. An 8th-century English monk's personal enchiridion. (Courtesy of the Stiftsbibliothek St. Gallen, St. Gall, Switzerland)	8
5	THE CLOISTER SCENE. Cuxa Cloister of the 13th century, reconstructed at The Cloisters, New York City. (Courtesy of The Cloisters, Metropolitan Museum of Art, New York)	11
6	THE CLOISTER WORKPLACE. St. Jerome at work in a cloister walkway, in a 12th-century illustration. (Courtesy of The Bodleian Library, Oxford)	13
7	THE SCRIBE'S PLEA TO HEAVEN. A 9th-century prayer at the commencement of a day's scribal labor. (Courtesy of The Bodleian Library, Oxford)	14

8	THE SCRIBE'S PLEA TO READERS. An 11th/12th-century commentary on scribal pain and reader politesse. (Courtesy of The British Library, London)	20
9	THE PLEA REPEATED. The heartfelt request of a 9th-century (?) French scribe. (Courtesy of The Bibliothèque Nationale, Paris)	23
10	SAFETY FOR THE SOURCE. Security measures for the monastic scriptorium, from a 10th-century illustration. (Courtesy of The Archivo Historico Nacional, Madrid)	38
11	THE PRE-MEDIEVAL LIBRARY. The storage of papyri rolls, from a 5th-century illustration. (Courtesy of The Biblioteca Apostolica Vaticana, The Vatican, Rome)	40
12	THE MEDIEVAL EXEMPLAR AND LIBRARY. The master copy and its means of storage, from a late-medieval illustration. (Courtesy of The Bibliothèque Royale Albert 1, Brussels)	41
13	THE BOOK PROTECTED. A medieval volume in full dress or chemise. (Courtesy of The Beinecke Library, Yale University, and The Metropolitan Museum of Art, New York)	44
14	A CURSE FOR A COFFIN. A 4th-century B.C. Phoenician curse to protect a priest and king. (Courtesy of The Istanbul Arkeoloji Muzeleri, Istanbul)	48
15	AN ANCIENT TEMPLE (LIBRARY?) CURSE. A 3800 B.C. Babylonian king's deadly threat. (Courtesy of The Museum of the University of Pennsylvania, Philadelphia)	51
16	THE OLDEST KNOWN BOOK CURSE. From a 7th-century B.C. Babylonian tablet. (Courtesy of Mr. Christopher Walker, Department of Western and Asiatic Antiquities, The British Library, London)	53

17	THE OLDEST COMPLETE WESTERN BOOK CURSE. From a 1st- or 3rd-century papyrus roll. (Courtesy of The British Library, London)	56
18	A CISTERCIAN'S SIMPLE CURSE. From a 12th-century manuscript. (Courtesy of Mr. H. Clifford Maggs, Maggs Bros. Ltd., London)	67
19	A BISHOP'S BOOK CURSE. From an 11th-century manuscript. (Courtesy of The Bodleian Library, Oxford)	72
20	THE CURATOR'S BOOK CURSE. From an 11th-century manuscript. (Courtesy of The Pierpont Morgan Library, New York)	74
21	AN EVISCERATING BOOK CURSE. From a 13th (?)-century manuscript. (Courtesy of The Vatican Library, Rome)	77
22	THE CHRIST CHURCH BOOK CURSE. From a medieval Apocrypha. (Courtesy of The Trinity College Library, Cambridge)	80
23	THE PRIEST'S BOOK CURSE. From a 12th-century manuscript. (Courtesy of The Harvard College Library, Cambridge)	85
24	THE ST. JAMES BOOK CURSE. From a 13th-century manuscript. (Courtesy of The Trinity College Library, Cambridge)	87
25	THE TWO SAINTS' BOOK CURSE. From a 12th-century manuscript. (Courtesy of The British Library, London)	89
26	THE CHARTER CURSE. From a 13th-century document. (Courtesy of Mr. H. Clifford Maggs, Maggs Bros. Ltd., London)	98
27	HER MAJESTY'S POSTAL CURSE. From a 20th-century envelope. (Courtesy of Prof. F. David Harvey, Exeter University, Exeter)	110

Permission by the above-mentioned individuals and institutions to publish these photographs is gratefully appreciated.

PREFACE

It seems to me sufficiently clear that wisdom is to be pursued for its own sake.
Mihi satis apparet propter se ipsam appetenda sapientia.
Servatus Lupus, Ep. i[93]*

It is not difficult to explain how it all began. I was once introduced at a lecture as a hopeless romantic who had fallen in love with the medieval alphabet. It was an oversimplification, but not much.

That early passion broadened to an interest in how medieval alphabets were used. To find out, I had to study original techniques, but that required first learning about who had employed the techniques—and that was made clearer by studying how medieval scribes had been taught the techniques. Research seemed to go in all directions. Who was this scribe? What were the books he worked on? Where did he work? What were his living and working conditions?

The result was my *Medieval Calligraphy—Its History and Technique*.† And what I thought then was the proper end of an affair proved to be merely the beginning. How can one stop being interested? *Medieval Calligraphy* mentioned a single book curse, and as my research

---

*Superscript numbers refer to the authors to whom I have turned for my research, whose names are listed in alphabetical order in *Sources*. To aid the interested reader, following each author's name is a list of all of his works I have read in gathering material for this book.
†Allanheld and Schram, 1980.

continued I found five, then ten, then more. It mentioned a few abecedarian sentences, but further reading revealed dozens. References to wax tablets, papyrus rolls, and vellum codices made me curious about their origin, mythical and otherwise, and more information surfaced. The brief description of scribal life fanned my interest in who these thousands of forgotten copyists had been. How were they schooled? Where did they work? As I dug further, the early medieval classroom came into focus, and with it the sound of students' complaints and the whack! of a palmer against an inattentive child. Who was the teacher? Why was he harried?

I studied monastic life to learn about the scriptorium, only to become curious about why scribes always moved their lips when reading. Researching this, I discovered their habit of speaking in hand-signals. Why? Each bit of information, answering one question, raised more.

I sit here in my study, two years later, surrounded by a bookcase of file boxes overflowing with cards of curious bits of information divided into dozens of categories: details of medieval scribal life, work, amusements, tools, techniques, book construction, classroom procedures, legends, anecdotes, details of script evolution. On the shelves are more than 800 books, journal articles, and xeroxes of unpublished theses from which this information was gathered. Among them are more than 400 other books and files of xeroxes containing an equal amount of detail which I get to as I can. It is my despair that reference material is always easier found than the time in which to digest it.

On my last visit to England I made my customary stop at Blackwell's Antiquarian Bookshop, housed in a lovely medieval manor in Fyfield, near Oxford. I was there, as usual, to visit my good friend Barry McKay, a consummate expert in antiquarian books, and to see what interesting volumes might have been acquired since my previous visit. My good sense having been blunted either by euphoria or the delicious meal we'd just finished at an ancient inn, I said, "I'll take that," when my eyes lit upon Sir William Dugdale's *Monasticon Anglicanum*.

There is nothing wrong, of course, with picking up another reference book. In fact, I tend to weigh the pleasure of any trip by the sheer dead weight of reference books under my arm at the trip's end. But this was different. Dugdale's research constitutes eight enormous books, the sum total in size and heft somewhat reminiscent of a sheep. A matronly sheep. It was a moment of happy madness that only a fellow book-lover, totally without common sense, can fully appreciate. Telling me a few days later that the set had been shipped to me,

Barry said he was in trouble with the management; the *Monasticon* had held down that end of the manor which now sat, sans Dugdale, at an unsightly tilt.

I wondered yesterday where, and how, the *Monasticon* can possibly be housed in my little study when it arrives. And since thought always (and dangerously, on my part) follows thought, I began to wonder about Dugdale and his history of the ancient abbeys, monasteries, hospitals, cathedral and college churches, etc., of England and Wales. Did it not all perhaps begin one unsuspecting morning in the 17th century when, with nothing better to do, he sat down in his study and decided to write something interesting about one unusual abbey? Had he intended only a mole-hill and not a mountain? Was my catalogue of filed notes the beginning of a monstrous work so compelling that it could not be stopped, and so large that few could—or would—purchase it?

The notes I've gathered are a delight to me, and I anticipate the pleasure of relaying them to anyone interested in ancient scribes and their books. But like two authors before me, I am compelled to insert a cautionary note. In the 12th century a scribe wrote out the *Tain*, the monumental Ulster saga of Cuchulainn (the Tain Bo Cuailnge). At its end he wrote

> But I, who have written this history, or rather fable, am doubtful about many things in this history or fable. For some of them are the figments of demons, some of them poetic imaginings, some true, some not, some for the delight of fools![63]

Present company excluded, of course. Five hundred years later, John Taylor inserted in his *Miscellanies*,

> All these things heer collected, are not mine,
> But divers grapes make but one sort of wine;
> So I, from many learned authors took
> The various matters printed in this book. . . .
> Some things are very good, pick out the best,
> Good wits compiled them, and I wrote the rest.

> If thou dost buy it, it will quit thy cost,
> Read it, and all thy labour is not lost.[76]

I must similarly remind you that I am a researcher and not a scholar. I have gathered together the truth as I could find it, and with it legends, apocryphal tales, and enticing bits and pieces only as reliable as the sources from which they come. They are all now a part of the fascinating perspective of medieval scribes and their books. But the past, as much as we may write of it, is a morass of confusion across which even a saint would hesitate to tread. In fact, take saints as an example: how does one, in writing about St. Colman, differentiate between the more than 130 by that name mentioned in Irish ecclesiastical records?[6] How does one know fact from legend when 66 different lives of St. Patrick were once in circulation at the same time?[78] (Let's not even look into the fact that the purpose of early medieval biographies was to make a religious statement, and only secondarily to relate factual data if it conveniently fit the purpose.)

So I sit here with Dugdale's manor-leveling works inexorably approaching, and my own growing daily. When I tried to carry the *Monasticon* from its shelf to Blackwell's shipping department, the subject of book curses came instantly to mind; and thus this odd bit of medieval past became the subject of this volume. May the reader find book curses as fascinating as I do.

> Some so-so things,
> Some bad, some good ones here,
> And that's the way a book is made, old dear.
> *Marcus Valerius Martialis*[55]

ACKNOWLEDGMENTS

O what a pleasant life it was, when we used to sit quietly among the learned boxes of books, amongst the abundance of volumes, amongst the venerable sentiments of the Fathers.

O quam dulcis vita fuit, dum sedebamus quieti inter sapientis scrinias, inter librorum copias, inter venerandos patrum sensus.

Alcuin, 9th century [93]

A researcher is only worth the books he is led to, the friends who support him, and the scholars kind enough to advise, correct, and occasionally translate. I hope this volume will reflect the esteem in which I hold those who have helped me: Cornelia Starks and Bruce Barker-Benfield, Bodleian Library, Oxford University; F. David Harvey, F. W. Clayton, and Mrs. Audrey Erskine, Exeter University, Exeter; Trevor Kaye, Trinity College Library, Cambridge University; C. B. F. Walker and R. A. H. Smith, The British Library, London; James J. John, Cornell University, Ithaca, N.Y.; E. G. Turner, University College London; Sister Wilma Fitzgerald and Paul Dutton, Pontifical Institute for Medieval Studies, Toronto; Peter Parsons, Christ Church, Oxford; Jan-Olof Tjader, Uppsala University, Uppsala; Mrs. George H. Semler, Jr., the Pierpont Morgan Library, New York; David Ganz, University of North Carolina, Chapel Hill; Julian G. Plante, Hill Monastic Manuscript Library, St. John's University, Collegeville, Minn.; Paul Meyvaert, The Medieval Academy of America, Boston; David Thomas and Richard M. Morante, Phillips-Exeter Academy, Exeter, N.H..

Also H. Clifford Maggs, Maggs Bros. Ltd., London; Raphael Posner, Jerusalem; J. B. (Barry) McKay, Blackwell's Antiquarian Bookstore, Fyfield, Oxfordshire; Christopher de Hamel, Sotheby's, London; Bruce Lewington, Weatherhead's Bookshop, Aylesbury, England; Roy H. Lewis, Bookfinders, London; Robert Fleck, Oak Knoll Books, New Castle, Del.; Emily and John Ballinger, The Book Press, Ltd., New Castle, Del.; Gunnlaugur S. E. Briem, London; Michael Gullick, Hitchin, Hertfordshire; Graham Newman, Bampton Castle, Oxfordshire; Michael W. O'Laughlin, Somerville, Mass.; Mrs. Anne-Rose Hertig, Mrs. Martha Drogin, and Gisela Hanstein Gaensler, Exeter, N.H.; Mark Van Stone, Portsmouth, N.H.; Marc Reeves, Chicago; Mrs. Margaret Broughton, Salford, England; Mrs. Dewey Henderson, Edmonds, Wash.; Russell Johanson, Seattle, Wash.; Mrs. Courtenay Willey, Pennington, N.J.; and Miss Judith Anne Duncan, Minneapolis, Minn., whose gift of her small volume first brought book curses to my attention.

I am especially indebted to the works of the late G. G. Coulton. They bring the Middle Ages to life because he chose, through contemporary quotes, to let medieval man speak for himself. When Coulton's own words were necessary, they were brief, clear, and to the point. In all my writings I endeavor to imitate a form of which he was an unsurpassed master.

Last, my thanks to the authors of the works in this and following sources sections. Friends are often busy elsewhere; scholars frequently disappear on lecture tours when you need them most. But these authors, by their works, are always at hand. They have become to me, through my years of reading, the source of my most-enjoyed hours.

I have sought for happiness everywhere, but I have found it nowhere except in a little corner with a little book.
               Thomas à Kempis (1380–1471)[23]

INTRODUCTION

We may wash and comb a dog as much as we will, yet it will still remain but a dog.

Ablue, pecte, canem, canis est, quia per maneat idem.

Lavez chen, peignez chen, toute vois n'est chien que chen.

12th-century Norman proverb[108]

So diverse are the details of medieval life that every author who approaches it can easily afford his reader a unique point of view. Had one the time to read everything, one might acquire an accurate picture. But one would also find contradictions everywhere. Whatever we try to make of the Middle Ages, the scope defies us. To reduce it to something we can easily comprehend, we lower our sights and attempt to grasp a particular area. The believer sees it as the childhood of Christianity; the warrior sees it as 1,500 years of intriguing and satisfying variations of bloodshed. The architect, the social scientist, the doctor or biologist sees it as the time of great awakening of what has become his own interest. And so each of us, by reaching for what we will, loses sight of the whole in acquiring a part. And if we wish to project a whole on the basis of that part, the distortion is inescapable.

It is no less a problem for those of us interested in the origin of our alphabet, of writing, and of the history of the book. But if our interest is, at this moment, the medieval scribe's curious habit of inserting curses in his books, perhaps we can understand this proclivity by starting with a broader view of the historic landscape in which it occurred. And attempt to see it not through our eyes, but through the scribe's, and learn about it as he himself described it.

It was not uncommon in the Middle Ages for dire curses to be laid upon books—in fact, the custom even bridged the gap from manuscript writing to printing. It is easy enough to quote the curses. But to understand how heartfelt such curses were, it would help to have a brief understanding of how books were produced, in what value they were held, what forces threatened them, and with what care—even resorting to the dramatic curse—medieval man attempted to protect them.

And so, on to the humble scribe, and how and why he brought down upon the reader of his books the *Anathema* or curse of excommunication and death.

> *You should make a habit in reading books to attend more to the sense than to the words, to concentrate on the fruit rather than the foliage* {qui soletis in Scripturis magis sensui quam verbis incumbere, fructui potius quam foliis inhaerere}.
> Notation in a 13th-century monastic chronicle (London, British Museum, Ms. Cotton, Vesp. E.4)[36]

ANATHEMA!

Plate 2

HOW BOOKS WERE WRITTEN

An incurable itch for scribbling takes possession of many, and grows inveterate in their insane breasts.
                    Juvenal (60–140 A.D.)[23]

          *   *   *

A monastery without books is like a state without resources, a camp without troops, a kitchen without crockery, a table without food, a garden without grass, a field without flowers, a tree without leaves.

Monasterium sine libris est sicut civitas sine opibus, castrum sine numerus, coquina sine suppellectili, mensa sine cibis, hortus sine herbis, pratum sine floribus, arbor sine foliis.
                    Jakob Louber, of the Carthusian Monastery in Basel[93]

For more than 1,000 years, the Christian Church, despite its excesses and incapacities, was a source—often the only source—of safety, serenity and culture in an often self-destructive world.

In the course of the Middle Ages, when the world often seemed to have gone mad, much can be said for the Church's role—what it stood for and what it did—in protecting and advancing what was good in mankind, and bringing it safely through to the Renaissance.

That you and I know about our past and can, at will, pick up a book and learn who we were and of what our culture was comprised, we owe in great measure to the Church. For if survival was its business, like any business it was supported in good part by paperwork. It could not operate, defend itself, or expand intellectually or geographically without enormous reliance on written material. It needed copies not only of God's word, but of the millions of words in commentary upon His: commentaries, sermons, moral tales, and lives of the saints (in a *Passionarius*). It needed copies of its own monastic rules (in a *Regula*), and then the histories of its communities (Chronicles) and records of their assemblies' decisions (*Consuetudinaria*).* It needed deeds and wills and letters to guarantee its legal position.† And it could not communicate among all its parts without letters from monastic house to Rome, and from monastery to monastery. Some things needed to be written only once, but for Catholic material (antiphonaries, bibles, canons, diurnales, epistolaria . . . see Appendix) there was a never-ending demand for copy upon copy. And when any work became antiquated, it was necessary to go back through it and *gloss* the manuscript to make it once again understandable.**

And not just Catholic material: much of what could be found from the cultures of ancient Greece and Rome was preserved and copied. Not because Church leaders were at all ecumenical when it came to pagan material at first.†† Pope Gregory once explained:

*The reader will find in the Appendix, A Confusion of Books, descriptions of the many different types of church-related books that might be found in use in the Middle Ages.

†It offered this service to outsiders as a means of occasional revenue.[12]

**Glossa* originally meant an unusual word, but later referred to the definition penned above it in minuscule writing. From collections and definitions of *glossae* we acquired the term *glossary*.[44]

††*Pagan*, as used here, and *heathen* mean non-Catholic. But both had similar origins having nothing to do with, or without, reli-

The devils know well that the knowledge of profane literature helps us to understand sacred literature.[71]

But it was perhaps more clearly put in a notation, shortly after 1025, in an Italian diary:

> Why does this reverent Abbot place the heathen authors, the histories of tyrants, and such books, among theological works? To this we answer in the words of the Apostle, that there are vessels of clay as well as of gold. By these means the tastes of all men were excited to study—the intention of the gentile writings is the same as that of the Scriptures, to give us a contempt for the world and secular greatness.[92]

The end result was that instead of being lost in the chaos of the early Middle Ages, the great works of Greece and Rome were preserved by copying and recopying. (It is a most appropriate term. To have a copy is to be enriched. It is from the Latin *copia,* meaning "abundance," that the French acquired *copie* and we took "copy.")[30] As the Middle Ages progressed, the ancient works were more and more appreciated. And it is only because of their having been copied in the Middle Ages that we know virtually anything of the history, philosophy, poetry, plays, or scientific pursuits of the Classical Age. The bridge between the ancient past and the modern age, then, was not forged by memory, but by the incredible and interminable process, hour after day after millenium, of copying books.

So important was the production of books that in the monasteries (the first and, for much of the Middle Ages, the only sanctuary of

gion. *Paganus,* in Latin, meant "peasant." In the Roman army a *paganus* was contemptible, a fellow who didn't enlist. It later came to mean a *heathen* or one who was not a soldier of Christ. Rather unfair, really: the *haethen* (Old English) was one who lived in the *haeth,* i.e., a country fellow whose only fault was that city dwellers, believing themselves more sophisticated, considered *haethens* to be uncouth.[30]

Plate 3: THE LABOR OF BOOK PRODUCTION. So important was book production that some monastic orders specified it in their Rules. That it was complex and time-consuming is seen in a set of nine miniatures from a manuscript produced in Germany, c. 1100–1150. Monks are shown (1) preparing parchment; (2) cutting it to size or scoring lines for lettering; (3) cutting a quill pen; (4) painting or trimming pages; (5) sewing the folios or quires together; (6) making the book's cover and (7) its clasp; (8) showing its completion, or its purpose in that one can learn from it oneself or (9) use it to teach others. (Bamberg, Staatsbibliothek Bamberg, MSC. Patr. 5 [B.II.5], folio 1 verso)

our culture) the tools for writing and the regulations regarding reading were an intrinsic part of the operating Rules (see Plate 3). In later years the production of books was specified:

> By this constitution we order that every monk not otherwise reasonably prevented at the time and place {appointed} be occupied in the study of reading, or in writing, correcting, illuminating, and likewise in binding books.
> *From the Statutes of the Benedictines.*
> *England, 13th and 14th centuries*[33]

> In place of manual labour the Abbot shall appoint other occupations for their claustral monks according to their capabilities {namely} study, writing, correcting, illuminating and binding books.
> *Ruling of the General Chapter*
> *of Canterbury, 1277*[33]

In early, primitive monastic communities, all members shared all labor, yet monasteries were not established for work, but for contemplation and prayer. As the community gained in size and wealth, an ever-increasing number of menial tasks were turned over to lay-brothers and employees. Writing was left to those most skilled at it, because of its importance. In the latter part of the Middle Ages much of this work was turned over to paid professionals, part of the sizable population of self-employed scribes who catered to businesses, private collectors, and the enormous demands for texts during the rise of the universities.

If we accept the all-pervading need to have books, we can begin to understand how much effort might willingly be expended by medieval man in acquiring and reproducing them. Any book, even badly produced and riddled with errors, might well be the only one on that subject that anyone in the community had ever seen. It was the result, in some cases, of weeks or months of negotiation with a distant house for its loan; the putting-up of a sizable pledge for its security; the wait for its arrival. And the copying of it, proofreading, decoration, and binding could involve months of labor on the part of several people. So highly valued was the act of loaning a book for copying that the house loaning its book would commonly ask that, for services rendered, the original be safely returned *plus* a copy.

In the latter half of the 9th century, Lupus, the Abbot of Ferrieres,* loved to borrow books so much that he was not above requesting copies from Pope Benedict III. When his victim understandably seemed unenthusiastic, Lupus insisted that the book in question was average in size and could easily be sent to him. But when anyone attempted to borrow a book from Lupus, he insisted that it was far too large or much too precious, or that the journey would be far too dangerous.[26]

We find it difficult today, surrounded by libraries, pestered by book clubs, tripped up in supermarkets by racks of books, to appreciate how rare a book was. Not so Apollinaris Sidonius. Hearing that a monk was passing nearby on his way to Britain with a particular manuscript, he rushed down the road with his secretaries, stopped the monk, and beside the road dictated the text to his staff.[80] Some monks who left their communities on pilgrimage and were given hospitality at a distant monastery are known to have stolen a book they found there;[4] the gaining of knowledge for their own community

---

*It is odd that an Aramaic word, *abba* (father), became abbot—the father of his flock, the head of his monastery (or abbey).[30]

was more worthy than the crime was sinful. And no studious monk abroad failed to carry his own *enchiridion* (notebook)* in which to jot down as much as he could of interest from every new book he found in his travels and which he could not afford to purchase (see Plate 4). So valuable were these "excerpts" that, to his fellows, they constituted a literary work in themselves.

Because of its reliance on books, the monastery devoted some of its space and much of its efforts toward the production of materials for and the copying of books. Good scribes were treasures. Odo, the Abbot of St. Martin's at Tournay in the late 11th century,

> used to exult in the number of writers the Lord had given him; for if you had gone into the cloister you might in general have seen a dozen young monks sitting on chairs in perfect silence, writing at tables carefully and artificially constructed. {Many important works} he caused to be transcribed. So that you would scarcely have found such a monastery in that part of the country, and everybody was begging for copies to correct their own.[18]

The study of the production of books (the evolution of the materials and tools involved, the location and furnishing of work areas, the rules regarding what was to be copied, who was to do it, and how it was to be done) is a lengthy and complex one. Only a few points need to be made here to make it clear that, stripped of its romanticism, the copying of books was a tedious and debilitating task, a mass-production effort. Even a brief knowledge of this will increase our understanding of how highly the end product was esteemed.

*See Appendix, *A Confusion of Books*.

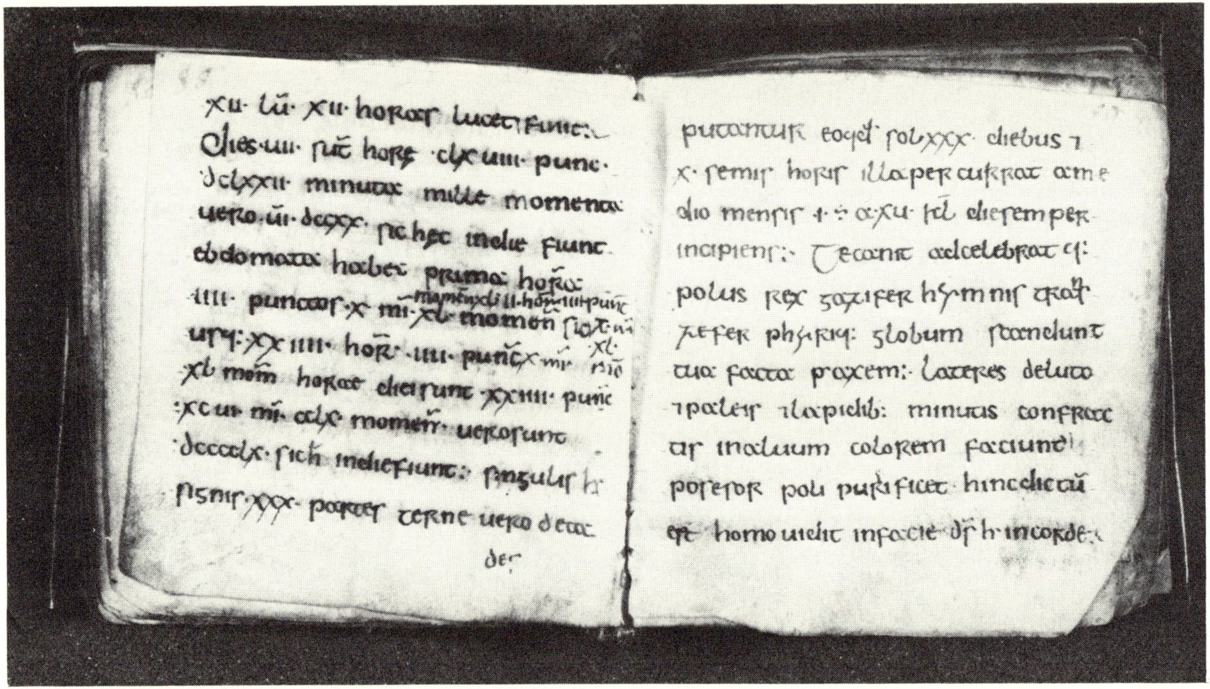

Plate 4: A MONK'S OWN BOOK. *Every monk in pursuit of knowledge carried with him a notebook in which he gathered, in order of acquisition, whatever he considered might be of later use. This enchiridion belonged to an English monk c. 780-90, who carried it while on a mission to Germany. One of its pages suggests that he was a teacher of young students or scribes, for it contains two Abecedarian sentences (see Marc Drogin,* Medieval Calligraphy *[Allanheld & Schram, 1980], pp. 12-13). (St. Gall, Stiftsbibliothek St. Gallen, Ms. 913, p. 89)*

From almost the beginning of monastic history, regardless of the educational value of books, their copying was considered manual labor and promoted as a way of involving the person in hard work for the benefit of his soul in the hereafter.[41] Although Abbot John Trittenheim of the Monastery of Spanheim lived at the end of the era,* his words would have rung as true almost a thousand years earlier. He urged his monks at their scribal work in 1486:

> I have diminished your labours out of the monastery, lest by working badly you should only add to your sins; and have enjoyed on you the manual labour of writing and binding books. These, and similar occupations, you may carry on with tranquility of mind and body, within the inclosure of the monastery. I wish that you may diligently perform even these works of your hands for the love of God, lest you eat the bread of idleness. There is, in my opinion, no manual labour more becoming a monk than the writing of ecclesiastical books, and preparing what is needful for others who write them; for this holy labour will generally admit of being interrupted by prayer, and of watching for the food of the soul no less than of the body. Need also urges us to labour diligently in writing books, if we desire to have at hand the means of usefully employing ourselves in spiritual studies.[54]

The monastic scribe was the soil in which his monastery grew and set out offshoots for, without him, it would wither and die. The scribe's was a menial task, but not menially perceived. Abbots found time to sit and copy. St. David himself began a copy of the Gospel of St. John, and St. Dunstan not only turned to such work frequently, but was famous for his skill.[33] Every hand that could write, did so.

---

*Trittenheim is more commonly referred to as Trithemius and was the author of *de laude Scriptorum* (In Praise of Scribes).

St. Columba, among his many works, copied a psalter. He might better have left it uncopied. It was borrowed from his teacher, Finian, apparently without permission. To copy without permission was considered embezzlement. Finian demanded back the original—and the copy as well. St. Columba refused, and the disagreement became so acrimonious that it reached King Diarmid. He ruled in Finian's favor, demanding the copy be returned with the psalter, "as calf must go with the cow." St. Columba and his followers went to war to regain it, and were forced into exile.[95]

The monastic scribe worked in far-from-productive conditions. In European and perhaps in Irish monasteries, an unheated room was provided for all to gather for copywork. In some cases, if the scribe were a ranking officer of the monastery, he might have his own simple workroom, and this was the case in later days with Carthusian monks.[26] The English monk engaged in writing, except in rare cases, had no writing room or scriptorium[14] (until at least the 14th century).[26] Instead he, like many of his contemporaries outside England, sat at a desk between arches of the covered walkway that surrounded the center of the monastic community, the cloister. Originally meaning any enclosed space, the *claustrum* later referred to the rectangular area formed by the surrounding walls of the monastic buildings, in the center of which was the garden or lawn, the cloister garth (see Plate 5). A logical architectural plan, it gave the community a center and allowed easy access to all the major structures. It also led to a feeling of being securely enclosed—and in some cases, unfortunately, trapped. It is from *claustrum* that the word "claustrophobia" derives,

Plate 5: THE CLOISTER SCENE. *The Cuxa Cloister, formed by the monastic buildings' placement in the 13th century as an open central area, appears a serene attraction to eye and mind. The cloister was the center of the monastery's activities, at one and the same time a haven and a confinement. Monks once flocked across the garth (or lawn, but in this cloister a garden) on various errands, while teachers taught and others met in the shadowed surrounding walkway, and scribes sat copying between the walkway pillars. (The Cloisters of the Metropolitan Museum of Art, New York)*

the fear of being enclosed,³⁰ which, on occasion, sent monks into a state of depression and even of violence.

The scribe's only protections from the elements were the ceiling, his clothing, and perhaps a screen between the arches. The English and continental scribe worked in relative silence (relative in that he recited aloud to himself the text which he was copying) with other scribes on either side of him. Beneath him was a backless stool and before him a severely tilted work surface (see Plate 6.) If there was no hurried need for a particular book, it was given to the scribe to copy from beginning to end. But when production speed was called for, the book was divided into sections, and a portion given to each of several scribes to reproduce. The scribe had no recourse should he wish to copy another, or not copy it at all. To object meant deprival of wine or even food at the end of the day. (To refuse meant greater punishment, in one case the extreme of being chained to his desk until the work was completed.)¹⁶ The material he copied might be of interest to him—but might well not. It could even be in a language foreign to him, which made the copying all the more difficult.

The weather might be uncomfortable, the light poor (no artificial light was allowed, for fear of damaging either the *exemplar* or the copy),* and the text difficult to read or tedious to contemplate. If the scribe were a monk still undergoing studies, he might well be questioned on the text when it was completed. Even if he were not, the threat of disapproval or punishment hung over him, because his work would be proofread by the elders (even perhaps by the abbot). To make an error was to commit a sin, for an error made and

---

*The *exemplar* was the master copy from which other copies were made. Great care might be taken that the copies were perfect in content, every word being proofread and even, in some cases, double-checked against its *exemplar*. Hence a most valuable, indeed *exemplary*, copy.

Plate 6: THE CLOISTER WORKPLACE. *The early 12th-century English illuminator Hugo Pictor, to illustrate St. Jerome in the act of writing, set the scene as it was most familiar to himself. St. Jerome is seated between arches in a cloister walkway. Only because saints deserve elevated status is he shown with a pillow for comfort and finer-than-functional seat and work-support. In England the cloister was, until late in the Middle Ages, the scribe's work center. Elsewhere in Europe the custom of establishing a scribe's room or scriptorium came into use much earlier. (Oxford, Bodleian Library, Ms. Bodley 717, folio VI recto)*

uncorrected would be copied again and again as others borrowed the book. An error-free exemplar was a monastery's treasure, sought after everywhere, as Odo well knew. In addition the scribe, in his copying, had to keep as closely as possible to a preset spacing so that his portion of the book would fit correctly in number-of-page sequence with those being copied by others to precede and follow it. And last, if he believed, religiously, in the power of his task, he knew that his labor with pen was the equivalent of another's with sword or battering ram: his was the responsibility of fighting the Devil by multiplying God's words. Not without reason, therefore, did some scribes as early as the 8th century begin their day's labor by penning a brief prayer, in the corner of their first sheet of parchment, asking for Christ's help (see Plate 7).[50]

It was also customary for the scribe to jot down, at the end of the manuscript, the title of the work, occasionally the place of copying, and even his own name. The space at the end of the manuscript was known as the *finit* ("end" in Latin), the *colophon* ("finishing touch" in Greek), or *explicit* (an abbreviation of the Latin *explicitus est liber*, "the book is unrolled," a phrase appropriate to its original appearance in the early papyrus rolls).[24] In time this was expanded to include a notation by the scribe regarding the religious enthusiasm with which he had undertaken the work. Once the precedent had been established, the scribes considered that space suitable for anything that came to mind: complaints, prayers, jokes, salad or face cream recipes,[97] amusements, puns, etc. Much of what we know of scribes is derived from their own words in their explicits.

Perhaps a century later, a scribe jotted down the following explicit:

Plate 7: *THE SCRIBE'S PLEA TO HEAVEN. So great were the scribe's responsibilities in terms of production and accuracy that it is understandable that he would look to a higher source for support. So, many 9th-century scribes began their day's book production by penning a brief plea (xb̄, the overbar indicating that the x and b were abbreviations—for Christe Benedic or "Christ bless"). (Oxford, Bodleian Library, Ms. Digby 63, folio 51 verso)*

> The art of scribes is hard compared with all other arts:
> the work is difficult, hard too to bend the neck,
> and plough the sheets of parchment for twice three hours.
>
> > *Ardua scriptorum prae cunctis artibus est:*
> > *Difficilis labor est, durus quoque flectere colla,*
> > *Et membranas bis ternas sulcare per horas.*[52]

If the pages of a manuscript were large and the text carefully written, it is estimated that the scribe's average speed was two to four pages daily. With an entire book copied on standard-size sheets, the average manuscript would have required three to four months' labor. A Bible might involve a year's work of six hours per day, six days per week. In the early Middle Ages the scribe was both letterer and illuminator; in the later days the two tasks were undertaken by different men. But a particularly fine manuscript complete with colored initials and miniature art work, done by a single scribe, could well take several years to complete.[4] (As a result, a library did not resemble anything close to our sense of the word. When Bishop Leofric took over Exeter Cathedral in 1050, he found its library contained only five books. He almost immediately established a scriptorium of skilled workers. By the time of his death in 1072, the crew had produced in the intervening 22 years only sixty-six books.[85] Similarly, the Monastery of St. Alban's recorded that swift work enabled its scribes to transcribe eighty works during the reign of Henry VI. Henry ruled for 39 years, hence St. Alban's scriptorium production rate was two manuscripts a year.)[61]

I hope I have not been misleading. Many scribes found joy in copying and have left heartfelt explicits that leave no doubt. But there was travail in achieving this joy, and many found nothing other than travail. We cannot know, for instance, how the scribe meant it, but we can read much into one little notation made by a late-medieval scribe in a margin of a manuscript of Aelfric's *De Temporibus Anni* (Cot. Tiberius B.V.). He undoubtedly wrote what thousands of others had felt:

God helpe minum handum![77]

THE CARE OF BOOKS—BESEECHED

Please wash your hands / Before touching this book.

Quisquis quem tetigerit / Sit illi lota manus.
  Note in a manuscript,
  Monastery of Monte Cassino
  (Cat. Monte Cassino, II.299)[13]

Perhaps no one would have a greater investment in a book than the scribe whose hours of toil and concentration produced it. Restrained from varying an iota in the copying of the text, the medieval scribe, once it was completed, was free to use his own words in asking that his work not be for naught. When we note the freedom of those words, his relief and anxiety are quickly revealed. As the scribe Florencio wrote at the conclusion of his copy of a manuscript in 945:

He who knows not how to write thinks that writing is no labour, but be certain, and I assure you that it is true, it is a painful task. It extinguishes the light from the eyes, it bends the back, it crushes the viscera and the ribs, it brings forth pain to the kidneys, and weariness to the whole body. Therefore, O reader, turn ye the leaves with care, keep your fingers far from the text, for as a hail-storm devastates the fields, so does the careless reader destroy the script and the book. Know ye how sweet to the sailor is arrival at port? Even so for the copyist in tracing the last line.[79]

While many scribes penned their wishes in brief, such as in a copy of a manuscript formerly in the library of St. Victor,

May this book never come near the hands of a man who doesn't know how to treat precious books decently.

> Qui servare libris preciosis nescit honorem
> Illius a manibus sit procul iste liber.[13]

most, by dint of profession, were never at a loss for words. Nor were they, again by the standards of their occupation, the least bit hesitant to copy others. A well-turned thought was admired and adopted. This fine art of taking another man's ideas and claiming them as one's own is an example of the different attitude that existed in the Middle Ages as compared not only with today, but with the Classical period that preceded it. Medieval writers felt that all the literature that existed in their time was a fund of man's knowledge, rather than belonging to its individual authors. A writer would borrow from a past work without care or concern in crediting its author—even if he knew who it was—and would then, often, not consider it important to sign his own work. Thus the difficulty modern scholars have in establishing who wrote what. In the Roman era such a concept would have been inconceivable. In the legal terminology of the Empire, the heinous crime of man-stealing was known as *plagium,* and a person who stole a child or slave, or tried to take a free person and sell him into slavery, was known as a *plagiarius.* That Martial would use such a term in describing the borrowing by one man of another man's words as his own indicates how severe a crime it was considered to be. *Plagium,* of course, became *plagiare* in French, and thus, in English, *plagiarism,*[71] and did not again become a crime until after the Middle Ages had passed.

With this prevalent attitude toward copying, it is not surprising that the pleas of scribes over the centuries began to take on a familiar tone. For instance, Prior Petrus, of the Spanish Monastery of Santo Domingo de Silos, wrote at his conclusion of the *Beatus Commentary on the Apocalypse,* circa 1091-1109 (see Plate 8):

> A man who knows not how to write may think this is no great feat. But only try to do it yourself and you will learn how arduous is the writer's task. It dims your eyes, makes your back ache, and knits your chest and belly together—it is a terrible ordeal for the whole body. So, gentle reader, turn these pages carefully and keep your finger far from the text. For just as hail plays havoc with the fruits of spring, so a careless reader is a bane to books and writing.
>
> *London, British Museum,*
> *Ms. Add. 11,695*[75]

Plate 8: THE SCRIBE'S PLEA TO READERS. When Petros, prior of the Monastery of Santo Domingo de Silos, at last completed his copy of Beatus's Commentary on the Apocalypse, he appreciated more than could anyone else the time and effort that the task had required. So, on the last page of the manuscript completed c. 1091–1109, he begged future readers to treat the book with care, and explained why in no uncertain terms. (London, The British Library, Ms. Add. 11,695, last page)

Since this is the second consecutive quote by a scribe who has assured us that life in the medieval secretarial pool left him at death's door, an explanation is in order. Researchers who are not calligraphers can too easily make the assumption that the act of writing was a physically superhuman task. In reality, the movement of quill upon vellum is effortless; and the act of lettering brings an instantaneous visual reward. The scribes' lament of external and internal disasters was a popular litany appearing at the end of manuscripts at least as far back as the last quarter of the 3rd century B.C.[65] The scribes were referring to the normal and understandable discomfort of sitting too long in an uncomfortable position, having to concentrate on material they may not have been interested in—or even understood—and the tensions of fearing to make an error and having to complete a given work in a specified time.

Or consider this anonymous scribe's conclusion to the *Silos Beatus* in the 12th century:

> The labour of the writer is the refreshment of the reader. The one depletes the body, the other advances the mind. Whoever you are, therefore, do not scorn but rather be mindful of the work of the one labouring to bring you profit. . . . If you do not know how to write you will consider it no hardship, but if you want a detailed account of it let me tell you that the work is heavy; it makes the eyes misty, bows the back, crushes the ribs and belly, brings pain to the kidneys, and makes the body ache all over. Therefore, O reader, turn the leaves gently and keep your fingers away from the letters, for as the hailstorm ruins the harvest of the land so does the unserviceable reader destroy

the book and the writing. As the sailor finds welcome the final harbour, so does the scribe the final line. Deo gratias semper.⁴²

If the words are not sufficient, consider the moment itself. Having finished a long and arduous task, the scribe could have put down his pen, leaned back, rested his eyes and refreshed himself before the next task at hand. But instead, he chose to stay hunched over his last vellum leaf to write yet another five or ten lines. Reginbert is a fine example: a gentle man, the Abbot of the Monastery of Reichenau, Germany, he had great affection and pride for the library in his care, and frequently added, at the end of the manuscripts he copied,

> In the loving name of God he swears an oath that no one give this work to anyone from outside unless that person gives his oath and pledge that he return safe to this house what he has taken. Dear friend, pay heed to the difficult effort of a scribe. Take me, open me, read me, do not harm me, close me and put me back.[15]

> *Adjurat cunctos Domini per amabile nomen,*
> *Hoc ut nullus opus cuiquam concesserit extra,*
> *Ni prius ille fidem dederit vel denique pignus,*
> *Donec ad has aedes quae accepit salva remittat.*
> *Dulcis amice, gravem scribendi attende laborem:*
> *Tolle, aperi, recita, ne laedas, claude, repone.*

Alas, history suggests that his plea was often unheeded.[15] And then there was poor Raoul:

Be careful with your fingers; don't put them on my writing. You do not know what it is to write. It is excessive drudgery; it crooks your back, dims your sight, twists your stomach and sides. Pray, then, my brother, you who read this book, pray for poor Raoul, God's servant, who has copied it entirely with his own hand in the cloister of St. Aignan.[80]

Here we see an added element. Messing with a scribe's work is one thing; messing with his Superior can be something else again. Some scribes, with justifiable fervor, brought the Almighty into the picture (see Plate 9):

Plate 9: THE PLEA REPEATED. *The 9th-century French scribe Warembert, a predecessor of Prior Petrus, felt a kinship of strain in book production. What gave him the severest post-partum blues after finishing his wearing task was the notion of a reader holding a page of the book and accidentally crumpling or ripping it. So he took the time to suggest that one's hands be kept safely about the covers of the book. (Paris, Bibliothèque Nationale, Ms. Lat. 12296)*

Friend who reads this, hold your fingers in back lest you suddenly blot out the letters; for a man who does not know how to write thinks it isn't work.[38] His latest line is as sweet to a writer as port is to a sailor. Three fingers hold the pen, but the whole body toils. Thanks be to God. I Warembert wrote this in God's name. Thanks be to God.

Amice qui legis, retro digitis teneas, ne subito litteras deleas, quia ille homo qui nescit scribere nullum se putat habere laborem; quia sicut navigantibus dulcis est portus, ita scriptori novissimus versus. Calamus tribus digitis continetur, totum corpus laborat. Deo gratias. Ego, in Dei nomine, Vuarembertus scripsi. Deo gratias.

                      From the 9th century[13, 69] (or 1523)[23] the Abbey of Corbie. Paris, Bibliothèque Nationale, Ms. Lat. 12296

"Three fingers hold the pen but the whole body toils" is perhaps the most popular occupational self-description in all scribal-explicit history. It appears with monotonous regularity in manuscripts, and can be traced back to a Greek papyrus-roll colophon of the 3rd century B.C. It was so familiar to scribes that it probably was inserted almost without thought, as seems to be the case here where it occurs near the end, as though it were remembered at almost the last moment. Normally it began or appeared early in an explicit, and was then emphasized by the familiar list of bodily ills. But this is the first example I have seen of its appearance accompanying a plea to the reader.

Other scribes invoked the protection of God even more explicitly. In a 14th-century manuscript from the library of St. Victor appears:

Whoever pursues his studies in this book, should be careful to handle the leaves gently and delicately, so as to avoid tearing them by reason of their thinness; and let him imitate the example of Jesus Christ, who, when he had quietly opened the book of Isaiah and read therein attentively, rolled it up with reverence, and gave it again to the minister.[13]

And, more to the point:

Take thou a book into thine hands as Simeon the Just took the Child Jesus into his arms to carry him and kiss him. And when thou hast finished reading, close the book and give thanks for every word out of the mouth of God; because in the Lord's field thou has found a hidden treasure.

Thomas à Kempis to his students[13]

These words indicate a wider range of concern because they were not appended by a scribe to a book he had just copied, but constituted the teaching of monastic, church, or general community elders. And such words of guidance in behalf of books spanned centuries and cultures.

The following words by Rabbi Judahben Samuel Sir Leon Chassid suggest a grim acquaintance with the mis-purpose to which books can be put.

Nor shall a man write any accounts upon the pages of a book or scribble anything on any part of it.

The Sefer Chasidon (*Book of the Pious*), *Regensburg, Germany, 1190*

He who loved and defended books, whether scribe or teacher, knew the potential of man's inconsideration. Richard de Bury, that most famous book-lover and collector of the later Middle Ages, knew exactly what might happen. In the *Philobiblon* which was written in 1344 either by him[33, 35, 106] or under his inspiration,[103] the horrors are recounted in Chapter 17 under the heading entitled *Of handling books in a cleanly manner and keeping them in order.*

> We hold that it is expedient to exhort students upon various negligencies which can be avoided but which are wonderfully injurious to books.
>
> In the first place, then, let there be a mature decorum in opening and closing of volumes, that they may neither be unclasped with precipitous haste, nor thrown aside after inspection without being duly closed, for it is necessary that a book should be much more carefully preserved than a shoe. But school folk are in general perversely educated, and if not restrained by the rule of their superiors, are puffed up with infinite absurdities; they act with petulance, swell with presumption, judge of everything with certainty, and are unexperienced in anything.
>
> You will perhaps see a stiff-necked youth lounging sluggishly in his study, and when the winter's frost is sharp, his nose running from the nipping cold drips down, nor does he think of wiping it with his pocket-handkerchief until he has bedewed the book before him with the ugly moisture.
>
> Would that he had before him no book but a cobbler's apron! His nails are stuffed with fetid filth as black as jet, with which he marks any passage that pleases him. He distributes a multitude of straws, which he inserts to stick out in different places, so that he may recall by the mark what his memory cannot retain. These straws, because

the book has no stomach to digest them, and which nobody takes out, at first distend the book from its accustomed closure, and being carelessly left to oblivion, at last become putrid. He is not ashamed to eat fruit and cheese over an open book, and to transfer his empty cup from side to side upon it; and because he has not his alms-bag at hand he leaves the rest of the fragments in his books.

Continually chattering, he is never weary of disputing with his companions, and while he alleges a crowd of senseless arguments, he wets the book lying open in his lap with sputtering showers. Aye, and then hastily folding his arms, he leans forward on the book with his elbows, and by a brief spell of study invites a prolonged nap; and then, by way of mending the wrinkles, he folds back the margin of the leaves, to the no small detriment of the book.

Now the rain is over and gone, and the flowers have appeared in our land. Then the scholar we are describing, the neglector rather than the inspector of books, stuffs his volume with firstling violets, roses and quadrifoils. He will next apply his wet hands to turning over the volumes, then beat the white parchment all over with his dusty gloves, and with his finger clad in long-used leather will hunt line by line through the page; then at the sting of the biting flea the sacred book is flung aside, and is hardly shut for another month, until it is so full of the dust that has found its way within, that it resists the effort to close it.

Especially, moreover, must we restrain impudent youths from handling books—those youths who, when they have learned to draw the shapes of letters, soon begin, if opportunity be granted them, to be uncouth scribblers on the best volumes and, where they see some larger margin about the text, make a show with monstrous letters; and if any other triviality whatsoever occurs to their imagination, their unchastened pen hastens at once to draw it out. There the Latinist and the sophister (one who pursues or transmits knowledge)⁶⁵ and every unlearned scribe proves the goodness of his pen, a practice which we have seen to be too often injurious to the best of books, both as concerns their usefulness and their price.

Nor let the crying child admire the pictures in the capital letters, lest he soil the parchment with wet fingers: for a child instantly touches whatever he sees. Moreover, the laity, who look at a book turned upside down just as if it were open in the right way, are utterly unworthy of any communion with books.

There are also certain thieves who make terrible havoc by cutting off the margins for paper on which to write their letters, leaving only the written text; or they turn to various abuses the flyleaves which are bound in for the protection of the book. This sort of sacrilege ought to be prohibited under pain of anathema.

Richard, in mid-rampage, still has a few segments of society to berate in a good cause:

It greatly suits with the honorable behavior of scholars that so often as they return to their study after eating, a washing should always precede their reading. Nor should a finger smeared with grease turn over the leaves or loosen the clasps of the book.

Let the clerk see to this also, that no dirty scullion greasy from his pots and yet unwashed shall touch the lilies of the books; but he that walketh without blemish shall minister to the precious volumes. Again, a becoming cleanness of hands would add much both to books and scholars, if it were not that the itch and pimples are marks of the clergy. As often as defects of books are noticed, we must quickly run to mend them; for nothing lengthens faster than a slit, and a rent which is neglected at the time will be repaired afterward with usury.[19, 33, 106]

THE VALUE OF BOOKS

When I get a little money, I buy books; and if any is left, I buy food and clothes.

Desiderius Erasmus
(1465–1536)[23]

* * *

[It is] far more seemly to have thy Studie full of Bookes, than thy Purse full of money.

Euphues[43]

In the preceding chapters we have seen books valued because of the time spent in their production, and as receptacles of knowledge, on which commodities it was difficult to put a price. But their value is even more easily assessed when one examines how medieval man dealt with his fellows when it came to his books.

No matter how far back one reads in the literature of the Middle Ages, one finds a passion for books; readers anxiously sought anything written on subjects that interested them.[67] Those who could copy books did so, regardless of the costliness of parchment. If for some reason the buyer could not make a copy himself, he might pay for the average book in his time what a collector pays today for a rare volume, finely bound.[80] Yet it is ironic what a small percentage of the book's cost went to the copier. The medieval scribe, even self-employed, usually received little pay for his work. The major portion of the book's expense was material (inks, brushes, paints, sheet and ground gold, vellum) and binding, covers, clasps, etc. In 1384, for instance, the illuminating materials and the illuminator's fee constituted five-sixths of the cost of Abbot Litlington's Missal.[81] The illuminator's fee and, even more so, the scribe's fee (after the early Middle Ages, specialization had set in and seldom were the two jobs done by the same person) were relatively insignificant sums. The average scribe in the later Middle Ages, for instance, had to work three to seven days for the sum earned in one day by a common foot-soldier slogging through Scotland in King Edward's army.[14]

At the end of the 15th century, even the advent of printing did little to reduce a book's price. It was more of a saving to buy parchment or paper, inks, etc., and copy a book than to purchase even a second-hand printed copy.[10] To build a good library, therefore, whether by purchase or copying, was enormously expensive. Credit Abbot Marchwart, of the Abbey of Corvey in North Germany, with a good idea: he made it a rule, when he was in charge late in the 11th century, that every novice who decided to join the abbey permanently must contribute a book to its library.[73] Abbot Raphael de Marcatellis, on the other hand, couldn't leave something that important to others. His solution proved that building a good library could be injurious to one's health. The head of St. Bavon's Abbey in Ghent (1437-1508), he spent so much attention on and diverted so much of the monastery's funds for the library that the upkeep of the monastery suffered, as became painfully obvious one day when the dormitory roof fell in.[20]

It is extremely difficult to report, in contemporary terms and/or contemporary coin of the realm, the price of a medieval book. First, a book's value at a given figure really depends on how hard one has to work to earn it, or what else one could buy for the price of the book. Second, surviving accounts of the value of books usually were written because the cost was so unusually high that it was worth mentioning. So existing reports invariably concern the most expensive. But a general feeling for books' value can be acquired from a few odd historical notes.

A Bible often represented a greater sum than the entire yearly income of a priest, and so very few priests were known to possess copies.[14] A parish priest in France in 1470, who felt compelled to own an antiphonary, paid a sum equal to the cost of 160 bushels of wheat.[93] Few could ever hope to own a newly printed Gutenberg Bible, for it cost roughly the equivalent of more than a dozen well-fed cattle or the title to a house in town.[40] Another account states that the average bound book of vellum pages at the end of the Middle Ages had a price tag equivalent to a month's wages paid to an average Neapolitan court official.[10] In 1331 King Edward III paid the equivalent of eighty oxen for an illuminated volume.[24]

Those who could not afford to pay in cash for books resorted to barter. A German nun, Diemude of Wessobrunn, penned a Bible which she traded, in 1057, for a farm.[68] An inscription in Latin written early in the 9th century establishes that the book in which it appears, the *Gospel Book of St. Chad,* written perhaps a century earlier, was taken in trade for the owner's best horse.[2] When a work on cosmography by Benet Biscop was admired by King Alfred, the author traded it to him for eight hides of land,[43] property sufficient in size to support eight families.*[78] The Countess of Anjou so much wanted a copy of the *Homilies of Haimon, Bishop of Halberstadt*, that she gave 200 sheep, five quarters of wheat and five quarters of rye.[33] When William de Longchamp, who later became Bishop of Ely in 1190, wished to raise funds to contribute to the ransom demanded for the return to England of Richard Lionheart, he didn't pawn a castle; he put up thirteen copies of the *Gospels*. And in the 11th[10] or 12th century[39] a Missal was known to have been traded for a vineyard.[10,33] Perhaps the greatest trade offered for a book was that made by a Bavarian official, who promised a monastic community the ownership of an entire town (in effect, the revenues from it, in perpetuity) in exchange for a single manuscript. After much consideration the offer was rejected, and not because it wasn't a fair exchange. The monks knew that the official could take back the town any time he wanted to—and probably would.[54]

People were, literally, willing to give their lives for books. An English schoolmaster, Geoffrey, living near the Monastery of St. Alban's, borrowed some books from that institution in the late 12th century—and watched in absolute horror as they were destroyed when his home went up in flames. As payment he offered to become a monk for the rest of his life.[40] In 1525 in Toulouse, a scholar's books were burned and the culprits were therefore condemned to hang.[47] In some communities toward the end of the Middle Ages, the penalty for book theft was death.[15] And it was not an idle threat.

*A hide has also been described as the amount of land a man could keep tilled in a year,[53] but it is really uncertain what is meant, since its definition varied in England from county to county.[58]

John Leycestre and his wife Cecilia were hung for stealing a book from Stafford church.[43]

When books were borrowed, pledges were taken, and if a book was not returned, there was hell to pay. In Poland, in the Renaissance, it was not unusual for the borrower to be taken to court.[95] When a book was purchased, therefore, it is understandable that it involved as much legal fuss as if the transaction had involved a house or land.[91] In fact, in the 14th century, the person selling the book, to prove (a) that he owned it and (b) that it was a copy free of error and unabridged, offered as a pledge not only all his worldly goods, but himself as well (*tous et chacun de ses biens, et guarantie de son corps meme*), and the pledge was witnessed by not one but *two* notaries.[71] Should the owner of a book fall upon hard times, he might be stripped of many things, but Jewish law from the 11th century onward forbade his being deprived of his book or books. The only exception was the case of a school teacher, who could seize his textbook.[70]

With this in mind we can see why, when a man died, he neither forgot to mention his books in his will nor simply mentioned their gift *en masse* to a friend or relative, as we might do today. In the Middle Ages, a book might not only be willed to a friend, but instructions might be included concerning who the book should go to after the friend's demise.[80]

The chamberlain to Pope Paul IV, Ulric Fugger of Augsburg, was so partial to books that he spent enormous sums in their behalf—so much so that his relatives went to court and had him declared incapable of managing his own affairs. Whether it was because his books were taken away, or simply because he could not buy another,

I cannot tell—but the result was that, in 1584, he died of melancholy.⁴³ His had been an extensive passion, but even the man who wanted only one book had sufficient reason to be melancholy about affording it. Wrote Robert Copland in the early 1500s:

> A peny I trow is ynough on bokes
> It is not so soone goten, as this worlde lokes.
> By saynt Mary I cannot tell the brother
> Money ever goeth for one thyng or for other.
> God helpe my fryende, this worlde is harde & kene
> They that have it wyll not let it be sene.
> *Seven Sorrows that Women have*
> *when theyr husbandes be deade*³

But, ah, to have a beautiful book enriched the soul. John Skelton, the poet and tutor to Henry VIII, wrote upon seeing the books around him,

> With that of boke lozened {diamond-shaped} were the clasps,
> The margin was illumined with golden railes {lines},
> Embiced {using blue or green pigment} and pictured with
>   grasshoppers and waspes,
> And butterflies and fresh peacocks' tailes;
> Englozed {glazed or made shining} with pictures well touched
>   and quickly,
> *It wold have made a man hole that had right to be sickly* {italics
>   mine}.³⁴

What had apparently moved him, as it does all of us when we are fortunate enough to first see an original example of such workmanship, was an illuminated manuscript—probably a Book of Hours.

How could such treasures, priceless in terms of labor, purchase value, content, and esthetics, be protected? The answer was by anathemas.

THE CARE OF BOOKS—DECREED

If a book has fallen to the ground, and at the same time some money or a sumptuous garment has fallen also, he shall first pick up the book. If a fire breaks out in his house, he shall first rescue his books, and then his other property. Nor shall he ever think the time spent upon attending to books wasted; and even if he finds a book so full of errors as that correction of them would be useless, he shall not destroy the book, but place it in some out-of-the-way corner.
   Sefer Chassidon, Regensburg,
   Germany, 1190[23]

The scribes who copied books begged readers to take care; elders lectured on and wrote about the value of books. But the concern went deeper, to the extent that the care of books became part of the Rule (operating regulations) of many monasteries. The following of these precepts had an effect not only upon the physical appearance of the monastic community, but may even have influenced their dress.

Early monastic communities often centered about tall stone towers built to protect the most precious items: monks, of course, and their books (see Plate 10). With the establishment of larger communities and therefore more complex structures, libraries were established. We must keep in mind that a sizable collection might range from two to twenty volumes. The library of treasures brought to England by St. Augustine in 597 consisted of only nine books.[61] The famous 12th-century teacher Bernard of Chartres owned only 24 books at the time of his death.[14] The Royal Library of Paris contained only four classics in the 14th century.[61] Richard of London, an abbot of Peterborough in the 13th century, had a private library of ten books.[43] At the same time in all England, there were fewer books than in the average library in 1933,[81] and the library of Oxford University consisted of a few books kept in a chest under St. Mary's Church.[61] The library of Cambridge University, remarkable for its 122 books in 1424, labored for a half-century to increase the number to 330.[10]

The evolution of ancient and medieval libraries is a sizable study in itself. In simplest terms, a library consisted of a box or trunk in which books were stacked (see Plates 11 and 12). In the Middle Ages, it became popular to store books in a wooden cabinet, not within a particular building but along the cloister walkway. So customary was this that one may still see today the recessed area of stone wall in which such a cabinet customarily stood in some monasteries. Within it the books were usually kept on their sides, not standing, and with their spines toward the back of the shelf because they were considered

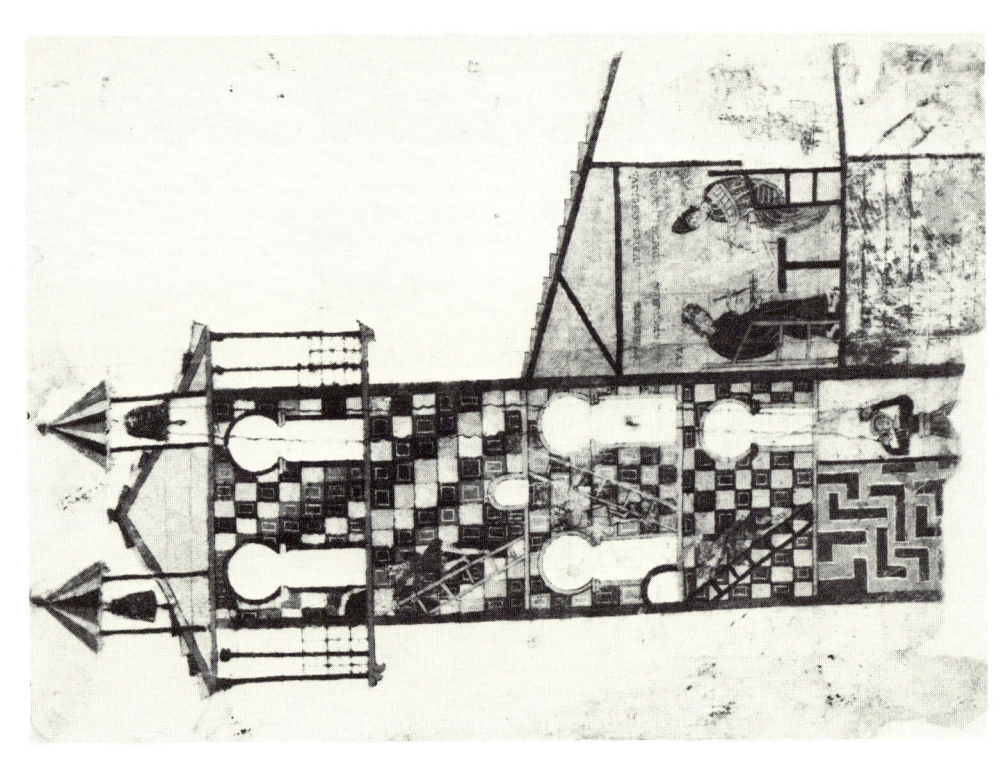

Plate 10: SAFETY FOR THE SOURCE. *If books were of value, those who produced them were no less prized. Completing a Beatus Commentary at the Monastery of San Salvador de Tabara in Spain in 970, the scribe and illuminator Emeterius illustrated himself at work, his assistant Senior seated across from him, and another assistant behind him, in the next room, cutting a parchment. All are on the second floor of a monastic tower building under maximum security;*[105] *bells can signal the alarm if an enemy appears, and ladders can be pulled up to deter access. This illustration was the model for a picture produced in 1220 in the Commentarius super Apocalypsum of Beatus of Liebana, produced at the Cistercian convent of Las Huelgas near Burgos, Spain (New York, The Pierpont Morgan Library, Ms. 429, folio 183; see Drogin, Medieval Calligraphy, Plate I). (Madrid, Archivo Historico Nacional, Cod. 1097B, folio 168)*

more important to safeguard than the edges of the pages, which faced the door. If a book was marked with its title, the title was occasionally penned across the surface of the ends of the pages, or burned into the edges with a hot iron.[94]

Books were not only bound for their protection, but further precautions were taken. Couchers and legers, because of their weight, could have their covers damaged when slid along a table. Because they rested on their back covers, the covers were given small legs (called *noduli*)[107] so that the back covers were kept clear of the surface. Because the leaves of books were vellum, and vellum left unconfined may buckle, it was advisable for books to be kept firmly closed, so each was often supplied with a clasp (called a *signaculum*).[107] Minor details, perhaps, but not overlooked by high Church officials whose task it was to visit area monasteries and churches to make certain that all was well. Returning in 1519 from a visit to York Minster, one such official reported unhappily that

> we fynde grete neclygense of ye decons and clerkis of ye vestre yt the mesbuke {Missale} is not clasped, whereby a fayre boke is nye lost.[107]

Oddly enough, few monastic rules mention or dictate, as part of community life, the production of books. The Rule of St. Benedict, in fact, orders no books to be copied but suggests it only by inference.* Yet almost every Rule, regardless of its length, is devoted in significant part to the caring for books.

> The library shall be in the keeping of the cantor. . . . When he is away, the succentor {sub-cantor} if he shall be fit for the office, shall

---

*It is obvious that the monks were intended to be involved in writing for, in a chapter discussing the fact that all possessions are the property of the community as a whole, appears the phrase "whether book or tablets or pen or whatever it may be . . ."[11] St. Benedict discussed manual labor at length; it is believed that he did not single out writing and copying because he considered it part of normal manual labor.

Plate 11: *THE PRE-MEDIEVAL LIBRARY. Before the creation of the codex (or book in the form we recognize it today) books consisted of long rolls of papyrus. In this manuscript c. 450–500, the author is shown seated between his desk and his library, a box capable of being securely latched, and holding what we may presume is a copy of the book in which this illustration appears. Romans with larger libraries constructed shelving so that rolls could be placed to rest in pigeon-holes. (Rome, Biblioteca Apostolica Vaticana, Ms. Vat. Lat. 3867, folio 3 verso)*

keep the library keys; but should he be giddy and light-minded, he shall give them to the prior or sub-prior.
Customary of the Monastery of Abingdon[33]

Whoever had charge of the case, or press, of books might easily become giddy simply from the responsibility. Books were often the community's most treasured belongings; complex rules existed regarding the loaning of books to and regaining them from the monks, who were often ordered to become familiar with specific texts through-

Plate 12: THE MEDIEVAL EXEMPLAR AND LIBRARY. *So valuable were books in the Middle Ages that more than one constituted a sizable collection; a library of books therefore might be no larger than—and usually was—a cabinet or small trunk. Of greatest value and most use was a copy known to be free of error, for it could be reliably used as the exemplar from which to make additional copies. Late in the Middle Ages, Philip the Good, ruler of the Netherlands, employed a professional calligrapher, Jean Mielot, shown here in a scene by contemporary illuminator Jean le Tavernier of Bruges. Note the exemplar safely positioned above the work-table and held in an open position, and the "library" behind the scribe's chair. If the work area seems uncommonly comfortable, remember that this was not a monastic scribe, and the "rewards" were not post-dated to the Hereafter. (Brussels, Bibliotheque Royale Albert 1, Ms. 9278-80, folio 10 recto)*

out a given year. For the Carthusian monks, a Benedictine offshoot that was established in 1084, the matter was clearly spelled out:

> Moreover he receives two books out of the press for reading. He is admonished to take the utmost care and pains that they be not soiled by smoke or dust or dirt of any kind; for it is our wish that books, as being the perpetual food of our souls, should be most jealously guarded, and most carefully produced, that we, who cannot preach the word of God with our lips, may preach it with our hands.[13]

Keeping after the monks was one thing, but the librarian had wider duties that posed greater danger:

> The precentor cannot sell, or give away, or pledge any books; nor can he lend any except on deposit of a pledge, of equal or greater value than the book itself. It is safer to fall back on a pledge, than to proceed against an individual. Moreover he may not lend except to neighboring churches, or to persons of conspicuous worth.
>
> *Customs of the Benedictine Monastery of Abingdon, late 12th century*[13]

While the day was laid out to allow time for the reading of books (indeed, Rules stipulated that when monks were busy at other tasks, such as dining, books would be read to them), and the physical layout accommodated the production and storing of books, a similar concern may have played a role in their dress. The long sleeves of monks' habits were so designed, it is said, either to cover their hands as a sign of humility, or to suggest that the monks' purpose in life was contemplation rather than physical labor—hence a sleeve unhandy for one who needed the freedom to use his hands. But one law suggests the possibility of another reason:

> When the religious are engaged in reading in cloister or church, if it be possible, they shall hold the books on their left hands, wrapped in the sleeve of their tunics and resting on their knees. Their right hands shall be uncovered with which to hold and turn the leaves of their books.
>
> The Traditio Generalis Capituli
of the Benedictines of England[33]

Brother Leot of Novara, having completed the copying of a text in the 10th century, was not concerned with which hand the reader used, as long as it was clean. Nor was he concerned about whether the reader sat or stood. Actually, he preferred that the reader not touch his book at all. Faced with the inevitable, however, Leot suggested the book be nestled in a protective layer of clothing (either the sleeve or another loose portion of the habit):

> Reader, turn the leaves gently, wash your hands, and if you must hold the book, cover it with your tunic.[26]

In similar fashion, the invention of the handkerchief led to instructions regarding books. When Italian monks objected to handkerchiefs as an effeminate accouterment, the monastic regulations of Monte Casino (established by St. Benedict) were amended to make a special ruling allowing their use not only for the expected purpose,

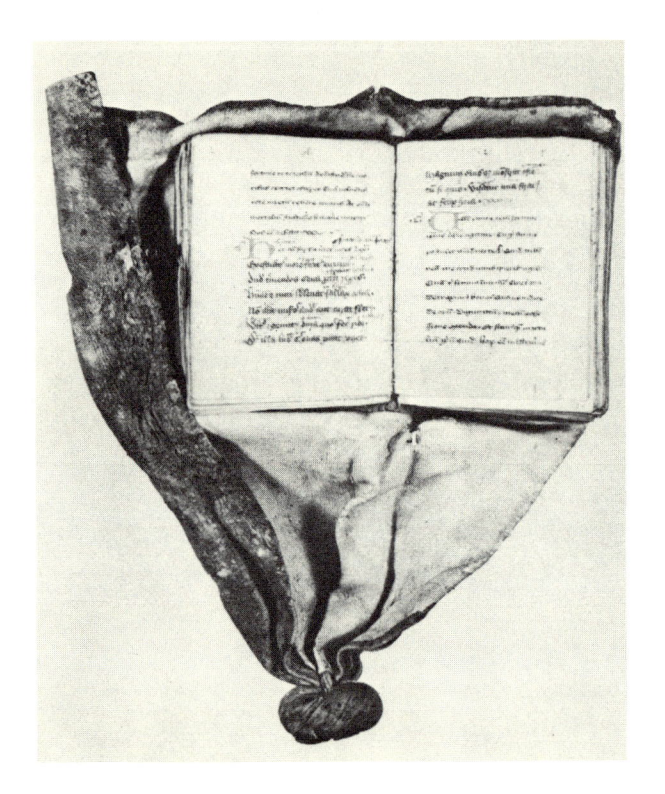

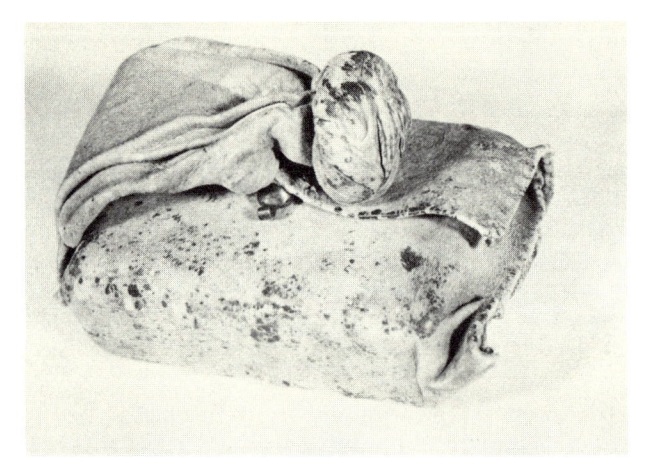

Plate 13: THE BOOK PROTECTED. *A manuscript was valuable and was therefore invariably protected by a hard cover. But the owner's concern often went further: a clasp to hold the book securely closed, and occasionally even "feet," or a stud at each corner of the back of the book so that, when it lay on a table, the book itself would be free of the surface. A simpler and more functional protection was the chemise, a cloth cover that not only wrapped itself securely about the book, but extended far enough beyond the book to be tied in a knot and slipped beneath one's belt so that the book could be taken about without fear of loss. (The Beinecke Library, Yale University; The Metropolitan Museum of Art, New York)*

but also "for wrapping around the manuscripts which the brethren handle," according to the Cat. Monte Cassino, II.299.[13] Other monasteries also required their inhabitants to hold their books in a sleeve or wrapped in a handkerchief.[80] Such wrapping was so sensible that occasionally books were bound in such a way that they could be wrapped in their own covers. The large covers not only could be folded over the front of a book, but were extended above the top of the book to such a length that the end could be tied in a knot. By slipping this knot under one's belt, a book could easily be carried about. A binding of that sort was called a *chemise* (see Plate 13).[37] The term today refers to a small portfolio that protects but is not an integral part of the book.[58] But in the Middle Ages it was part of the book itself and popular not only as a protective measure but as a means of easily keeping a treasured possession safely at hand. This is clear, for instance, from the wording of a portion of a late 15th-century will in which a doting father ordered

> that my doughter lady ffitzhugh have a boke of gold, enameled, that was my wiffes, whiche she was wounte to were {wear}.[107]

Poor Lady Ffitzhugh and ffolk like Ffawkes and Llewellyn and Lloyd; all suffered from typesetters' misunderstanding. In gothic times the capitals F and L were designed with each repeated to give the finished capital letter form more strength. When printing came into vogue the handwritten capitals were misinterpreted as FF and LL instead of F and L, and therefore were set in type as Ff and Ll.

ANATHEMA!

I am the guardian of the letters. . . . Keep off.
                                                    1st century[83]

So precious were books in the Middle Ages that any measure taken to protect them was welcomed. Once a book had been produced, it was carefully catalogued and locked in a secure place, with the keys kept by a most responsible official. Monastic community regulations specified in detail how books were to be guarded, who was to be responsible for them, how the reader was to borrow them, and the procedure for their return after a specified amount of time. To loan a book to someone outside the monastery walls was considered, by some, equivalent to throwing it away. If a book had to be loaned, a heavy pledge was placed against it. But no pledge, to some, could compensate for the loss of a book, and several communities passed strict laws prohibiting any loan under any circumstances.[71]

Outside the monastic walls, the book was no less valued. With the rise of universities and a heightened literacy rate in the later Middle Ages, the classical concept of school and public libraries was reintroduced. But so precious were the few books in any library's collection that each was protected by rules and regulations. Richard de Bury, although familiar with what could happen to books, donated some to Oxford University—but demanded that, in return, it be firm policy that no book could be loaned out unless a duplicate copy was safely shelved.[43] To many people even this was insufficient, and it became customary in many libraries to secure each book to the shelf or reading table with heavy lengths of unbreakable chain. The notion of a "lending library" was in most cases inconceivable.

But how does one find the ultimate protection for a book? Any book can be stolen and, even if it is chained to a desk, what can protect it from smudges, stains, unwelcome notations or, most tragic, the ripping out of a particularly interesting page? Medieval man had the ultimate solution: he who had placed his existence in the hands of the Almighty decided that there was room there for his books as well. And so they were placed under God's protection—a Librarian few if any would be foolhardy enough to cross.

The concept of placing an inanimate object under the protection of a diety must be as old as man's first acquaintance with or creation of his god(s). From the first, that relationship established gods with powers over man, and man asking their aid and protection. Surely one of the earliest requests was that man be aided and protected not only from Nature and Fate, but from a most dangerous enemy—his fellow man. A religious man was the stronger for the gods to whom he prayed, and could threaten others or be protected from others with the gods' power. Hence the concept of a curse may be as old as religion itself. And if man sought protection during his lifetime, he was known to have sought it as well for his mortal

Plate 14: A CURSE FOR A COFFIN. *Man's ability to threaten his fellow man with the awesome power of his gods has been a benefit of religion since the most ancient of times. Our ancestors may have thought to place God's curse on their books because they had even earlier been accustomed to placing God's curse on something they valued even more— themselves. In the 4th century B.C., the king of Sidon departed this vale with a curse not upon his lips, but upon his coffin. (Courtesy of the Istanbul Arkeoloji Muzelen, Istanbul, Turkey)*

remains when his life's span ended. Curses laid against the desecration of burial sites are known from the most ancient times; those of the pharaohs of Egypt are a case in point. Less familiar, but most eloquent, is that of a king of Sidon (see Plate 14), who died about 350 B.C. and upon whose coffin, now in the Istanbul Arkeoloji Muzelen, is inscribed

> I, Tabnith, priest of Ashtart, King of the Sidonians, son of Eshmunazar, priest of Ashtart, king of the Sidonians, lie in this coffin. My

curse be with whatever man thou art that bringest forth this coffin! Do not, do not open me, nor disquiet me, for I have not indeed silver, I have not indeed, gold, nor any jewels of . . . only I am lying in this coffin. Do not, do not open me, nor disquiet me, for that thing is an abomination to Ashtart. And if thou do at all open me, and at all disquiet me, mayest thou have no seed among the living under the sun nor resting place among the shades![56]

Two thousand years later, William Shakespeare caused to be engraved on his tomb at Stratford-on-Avon:

> GOOD FREND FOR IESVS SAKE FORBEARE,
> TO DIGG THE DVST ENCLOASED HEARE:
> BLESE BE Ɇ MAN Ṯ SPARES THES STONES,
> AND CVRST BE HE Ṯ MOVES MY BONES.[56]

Of course, man was concerned with his own remains before thought of his books occurred. At any rate, the idea of protecting what was his with the vengeance of God was not a new concept when man reached a stage in which he had books and worried about them.

Historians suggest that the idea of book curses originated with Eastern manuscripts. The ingredients for godly intervention certainly existed from the very beginning of writing. Perhaps without exception, every civilization which created for itself a form of writing felt that the skill had originated as a direct gift from superhuman sources. We who are so accustomed to reading cannot truly comprehend the awe with which early man viewed his new-found ability to take the spoken word and make it (a) visible, (b) capable of storage, and (c) able to be spoken again at any future time. Because the magical art of writing was a gift from his god(s), and because only the most-educated of men could comprehend it—and they were the priests—the earliest writings were invariably religious; the sacred and most-holy secret writings of that civilization. As such they were kept in the temple and protected by the gods.

What may well be the oldest such curse we know is now almost 6,000 years old. I say *may be* because it protected the temple's "library" only by implication (see Plate 15). The curse was inscribed on the temple's door socket (now in the museum of the University of Pennsylvania) by order of Sargon I, who ruled Nippur, in Babylon, c. 3800 B.C.:

> Shargani-shar-ali [Sargon], son of Itti-Bel, the mighty King of Accad and the dominion of Bel, the builder of Ekur, the Temple of Bel in Nippur. Whoever removes this inscribed stone, may Bel and Shamash tear out his foundation and exterminate his posterity.*[56]

A nasty prospect to imagine one's foundation being torn out, let alone having one's posterity exterminated. Actually, the curse may have been as deadly as it was sincere. The record is confusing, but when King Nabonidas ordered excavation work for renovations 3,450 years later, it may have been at the site of this same temple. If indeed it was—and if he disturbed the foundation—it is interesting to note that Nabonidas *was* the last king of Babylon.

About 3,000 years after Sargon I had cursed his way into history,

ANATHEMA! 50

*Bel, perhaps more familiar as Ba'al, was the *Father of the Gods*; Shamash, the *Sun God*, was also considered the embodiment of Justice.[27]

a similar custodial concern was offered in behalf of Darius, one of the kings of ancient Persia. Carved in rock at Behistun is the following inscription:

> Thus saith Darius the King: If thou seest this panel or these figures and destroyest them, . . . may Ahuramazda smite thee, may thy family come to nothing; whatever thou doest, may Ahuramazda destroy it.*[32]

The ancients had a refreshing way of wasting few words while simultaneously expressing ultimate concepts.

While collections of Egyptian religious writings can be found as far back as 3200 B.C., they are no older than the Egyptian belief in Thoth, the god who created writing. All books, and consequently all temple libraries, were under his guardianship. While there is no evidence of his stipulating a curse against anyone damaging or removing his books, there is ample written evidence of his specifying

*"Ahuramazda" means the *Wise Lord* or *Good Spirit*.[27]

Plate 15: AN ANCIENT TEMPLE (LIBRARY?) CURSE. As early as 3800 B.C., if not earlier, the curse was employed in protection of books—if one accepts a temple curse as applicable to its holy volumes. This curse on the door socket of the Temple of Bel, ordered carved there by King Sargon I (c. 3800 B.C.) may be the world's oldest surviving book curse—mincing no words and damning the miscreant, his past, and his future. (Courtesy of The Museum of the University of Pennsylvania, Philadelphia)

exactly who he was, and one can presume that it was quite clear that he was not to be irritated:

> I am Thoth the perfect scribe, whose hands are pure, who opposes every evil deed, who writes down justice and who hates every wrong, he who is the writing reed of the inviolate god, the lord of laws, whose words are written and whose words have dominion over the two earths.
> *The Book of the Dead*

While a god ruled from above, he who ruled on earth was, as king, a god himself. Pharaoh, for instance, was at the same time god and king; as we advance to the Western world in the Middle Ages the king ceased to be god but at least ruled by Divine Right. Books that in earliest times belonged to god belonged as well to the king, being one and the same. As time progressed and the authority of the religious and civilian authority diverged, the few books which existed outside the temple were invariably inside the court. And what may be the earliest surviving curse to specifically mention books protected the library of clay tablets belonging to King Assurbanipal (668–626 B.C.) who ruled Babylon, the capital province of Assyria. His curse is found repeated on most of the tablets (see Plate 16):

> The palace of Ashur-bani-pal, king of hosts, king of Assyria, who putteth his trust in the gods Ashur and Belit* . . . I have transcribed upon tablets the noble products of the work of the scribe which none of the kings who had gone before me had learned, together with the wisdom of Nabu insofar as it existeth {in writing}. I have arranged them in classes, I have revised them and I have placed them in my

*Supreme earth god and goddess.[27]

palace, that I, even I, the ruler who knoweth the light of Ashur, the king of the gods, may read them. Whosoever shall carry off this tablet, or shall inscribe his name on it, side by side with mine own, may Ashur and Belit overthrow him in wrath and anger, and may they destroy his name and posterity in the land.[15, 95]

Far more is implied by "destroy his name" than the simple threat of "being forgotten." One must remember in what great awe the written word was still being held. The Egyptian gods had been so much a part of the words written by or about them that they were the words themselves. The name of a god *was* that god. In religious processions, the carrying of his written name constituted his actual presence.[74] To erase anyone's name was not to remove the recollection of him, but to cause him to have ceased to exist, the reason for the

Plate 16: THE OLDEST KNOWN BOOK CURSE. *While the book curse can be traced back into the 39th century B.C. by the temple curse's association with the temple contents, the curse specifying books is certainly at least as old as the 7th century B.C. Perhaps the oldest known true book curse was ordered inscribed on innumerable clay tablets by the ruler of Babylon, King Assurbani-pal, who was concerned not only with his books' safety, but with the credit due him for having ordered their production and collection. This tablet, from Ninevah, contains an almost complete curse.*[99] *(Tablet K 155, courtesy of Mr. Christopher Walker, Department of Western and Asiatic Antiquities, The British Library, London)*

chiseling off of certain pharaoh's names from cartouches and other stone, such as occurred after Akhenaton's death. Given the attitude in nearby Egypt at that time, it is safe to presume that Assurbanipal, in Babylonia, was offering to have his gods not only kill the transgressor, his children, and their children, but void no less than the existence of his ancestors. This is indeed "rage and fury." (While damning one's past may at first seem a sophisticated, if not philosophical concept, consider this: to tell a Maori "go and cook your father" is considered a great curse, but minor compared to "go and cook your great-grandfather," because it implies wiping out the designated chef's entire ancestry, self, and future.)[18]

When such a curse came into use in the Western world is not known. But more than 300 years passed before the first surviving indication. Sometime in the last quarter of the 3rd century B.C., a Greek scribe finished copying a papyrus of a portion of Menander's *Sikyonios* and jotted down what is, today, the oldest known Greek colophon. What remains of the three lines is

>   Do not jeer at the script . . .
>   Of he who jeers at his leg . . .
>   {paragraph mark}
>   {So happily} I rest my thre{e fingers}.[65]

It is certainly incomplete, and the meaning is unclear. But some scholars believe it could be a curse against the roll's mishandling.[65] Might the scribe, having asked the reader not to jeer, then gone on to explain what would happen if he did?

As mentioned earlier, this is the oldest surviving mention of the use of three fingers to hold the pen (an extremely popular reference throughout the entire Middle Ages); we also note mention of the act of writing, and the leg, which suggest the familiar medieval plaints. But instead of the scribes crediting writing with pain to their eyes, backs, chests, bellies, ribs, kidneys, and viscera, this is an attack below the belt. The reason is quite simple: the medieval scribes worked at desks and/or tables; here we deal with scribes who were, among other things, their own desks. The Greek and Roman scribe sat on a stool or bench, his legs bent before him and both feet firmly on the ground, or possibly with the right foot resting on a footstool to elevate it slightly. With the papyrus draped across his lap, he wrote on the area of papyrus that lay across his right knee.[60, 65] Thus he might well complain of pain in leg and/or knee—not from pressure of pen on papyrus, but from having to remain still for great lengths of time. Had he been an even earlier scribe, say an Egyptian who customarily sat cross-legged on the ground, the complaint would have centered on a more-fundamental area.

A clearer example, 500 years later and still more than 500 years before the earliest Christian example, survives in a papyrus roll (the earliest form of the book as we know it today). The roll, containing the third and fourth books of the *Iliad* in Greek, now rests in the British Museum. On a separate sheet at the end of the roll (see Plate 17), the scribe, sometime in the 1st century A.D.[83] or 3rd century A.D.,[65] wrote:

> I am the guardian of the letters.
> The reed pen wrote me, the right hand and the knee.
> If you lend me to someone, take another in exchange.

Plate 17: THE OLDEST COMPLETE WESTERN BOOK CURSE. While the book curse apparently originated at a period of book evolution in which the book consisted of clay tablets, the oldest known complete book curse of Western origin was penned when that evolution had reached the stage of papyrus rolls. Here, in this earliest known example from the 1st or 3rd century A.D., the reader is warned against erasing the text, and the implication may well be that he would risk being erased himself. (London, The British Library, Papyrus 136, separate sheet at the end)

If you rub me out, I will slander you to Euripides.
Keep off.

> *London, British Museum,*
> *Papyrus 136*[83]

It is extremely difficult to be certain of precise meanings in ancient Greek, so I include a second translation:

{The colophon speaks:}
  I am the flourish, protector of the scribes
  A reed wrote me, with a right hand and a knee
{The book speaks:}
  If you use me for anything, assist another*
  But if you smear me, I will slander you before Euripedes,
    so desist.

*I.e., as I have helped you, be helpful yourself.

Here we are without doubt dealing with a curse, and this particular one may well be the oldest complete book curse surviving from Western antiquity. The Euripides mentioned is probably the 5th-century B.C. tragedian.[38] While it is true that news tended to travel slowly in the old days, 500 years or more surely should have been sufficient for word to get to the scribe who wrote this curse, and he could not possibly have assumed that Euripides was in any condition to listen to gossip. So whatever point he *was* trying to make by referring to Euripides is unfortunately lost to the ages.

It is interesting that, while the third line of the second translation suggests a humanitarian ideal, the same line in the first translation is purely practical, reminding one of the medieval concern for books:

take another book as collateral against the loan of this one if you ever expect to see it again. Whatever one may read into it, this curse in defense of the defenseless book well represented all that was to follow.

With the coming of Christianity, the tradition of protecting books and libraries continued. In Western eyes and hearts the power to protect no longer rested with Thoth, King Assurbani-pal, Ashtart, Ashur or Belit, Bel, Shamash or Ahuramazda, but with a source mightier than all who had come before: God Almighty. As Western monastic communities were established, many not only promulgated laws against lending books, but formally placed them under God's protection by stating that anyone posing a threat to them would receive the ultimate punishment—the curse of excommunication.[71] The earliest surviving example of such a curse occurred in a manuscript produced in the Monastery of St.-Denis in 627.[95]

Excommunication, the ultimate threat, first appeared in Church documents in the 4th century.[53] It consisted of the complete rejection of a person from all association with the Church, from relationship with its flock, and from any possibility of salvation in the Hereafter, and declared him to be the property of Satan[64]—while at the same time keeping him bound to all religious duties.[53] In a chaotic world where the Church and monastery might well offer the only security, or humanity, known to medieval man, it could be considered—even by a man not wholly religious—a death sentence.

It was virtually impossible for someone to be unaware of the threat of excommunication, for that "Great Sentence," as it was called, although it had no official position in any Service book, was reproduced in varying lengths in some Manuals, and was ordered to be read aloud to the congregations not once or twice but four times a year. Hence the preamble:[107]

> The grete sentens I wryte thee here,
> That foure tymes in the yere
> Thou schalte pronownce with-owtyn lette,
> Whan the parich is to-gydur mette;
>
> Thou schalte pronownce this hydowse thinge
> Wit cros and candul and bell knyllynge,
> The furste sononday affter myghell feste;
> Mydlenton sonday schal be neste;
> The trenite feste is the thridde, os I thee say;
> The ferthe is the sononday aftur candulmes day.[107]

On each of those four days, as every living soul sat hushed, God's representative intoned the Great Sentence:

> Be the auctorite of our lorde ihesu cryste . . . we denownce accursed & owte of the company of god & off alle holy chyrche . . . Alle that leyne hand on preste or clerke or of man or woman . . .

and the list of excommunicable misdeeds rolled on and on until the "hydowse thinge" itself was pronounced, by the authority of the Father, Son, and Holy Ghost:

> we acurson and waryon {denounce} And departon {divide} from alle gode dedus & prayeres of holy chyrche, and dampnon in-to the peyne

of helle, Alle yoo that have done theis articoles . . . We acurson hem . . . sclepynge & wakynge, goynge, syttynge and standinge . . . spekynge rydynge . . . etynge, drynkynge, in wode, in watur, in felde & in towne . . . tyl they comen to amendemente & satisfaccion made. fiat, fiat! amen.[107]

Because it was so "grete" a sentence that it would strike its victim no matter what task he was about, and no matter where he might be, for all time, it was at first used sparingly. But the *anathema*, as the curse is known in Church Latin, came to be used more and more until the word itself began to mean any curse.[31, 65] Today, the medieval book curse, whether or not it specifies excommunication, is commonly referred to as a *book curse*, a *malediction*, or an *anathema*, the term I favor.

In the 19th century and earlier it was believed that the anathema was instituted as a matter of medieval, official, Church policy specifically as a book curse. As evidence, proponents point to a notation by Bernhard of Montfaulcon, a monk in the 14th century. After completing the translation of a psalm, Bernhard added a warning presumably against anyone who would damage or steal the manuscript: that he or she would receive the curse of all 318 Nicean Fathers, and the Trinity, the Mother of God, John the Baptist, *and* all the saints. To prevent any possible uncertainty, Bernhard also promised the miscreant the fate of Sodom and Gomorrah, and the rope of Judas Iscariot. (Since Judas hanged himself, the reference is either to being hanged or to being driven by remorse to suicide.)

Impressed as they may have been with Bernhard's over-kill, it must be said that scholars were less interested in the Trinity, the Mother of God, John the Baptist, every blessed saint, and the ultimate in urban renewal than they were in the Nicean Fathers. Had the Council of Nicea instituted an official policy regarding anathemas? It would appear so—for many miles and years away a Syrian scribe named Nectarius, concerned for the safety of a manuscript he was copying (Cod. Ambros. 89), jotted down an anathema in which the disaster-du-jour of leprosy—apparently not sufficiently threatening—was accompanied by the disfavor of the Holy Fathers of the Council of Nicea.[32] Nevertheless, historians have found that the council set no policy regarding anathemas.[15]

But if one came away from Nicea thinking Mother Church had no policy on the matter, it was contradicted by a get-together in Constantinople in 719, when the Third Council enacted a canon which held

> That nobody whatever be allowed to injure the book of the Old and New Testament, or those of our holy preachers and doctors, nor to cut them up, nor to give them to dealers in books, or perfumers, or any other person to be erased, except they have been rendered useless by moths or water or in some other way. He who shall do any such thing shall be excommunicated for one year.[73]

Perfumers may seem an odd stratum of the commercial world to single out for attack, but they historically bore the sweet smell of biblioclasm or book destruction. In earliest times when it was discovered that burning papyrus gave forth a pleasing aroma, perfumers created incense cornices from the pages of discarded books (at that time rolls).⁴⁹ When parchment replaced papyrus, perfumers and others used pages of books to wrap goods for their customers.

At the Council of Paris in 1212 it was decreed that

> From the present date, no book is to be retained under pain of incurring a curse {i.e., stop trying to scare off potential borrowers by laying anathemas}, and we declare such curses to be of no effect.⁹⁵

The only conclusion it is safe to draw (aside from the obvious one that attending too many councils can shake one's faith in Catholic continuity) is that official policy depended on where one was and when, if there were a policy and, inevitably, if one chose to conform. In other words, we simply cannot be sure, but it would appear that no single policy was universally in effect for any majority of the Middle Ages. But Mother Church certainly offered an environment conducive to anathemas. They had been employed for centuries and were compatible with the Church's attitude; for if the Church offered Eternal Life to those who produced books, why would it be unreasonable to deny Eternal Life to those who would destroy books?¹⁵ Individual monasteries may have favored or deplored their use; but the decision to insert an anathema, and its subsequent detail, length, and creativity, seems to have been primarily the decision of the scribe.

Most anathemas were laid against borrowing or lending,³⁰ but no crime was too small. The prior and others in the convent of Rochester are known to have pronounced the sentence of damnation on anyone who not only stole or hid, but even erased the title of their Latin translation of Aristotle's *Physics*.[80]

An anathema, as we have seen, could exist in two forms. The first was a protective curse placed over all the books of a given library. But even if it is not only pronounced but posted on the library door or wall, how is one to know that the reader will have it firmly in mind once he is alone in his room with the defenseless book at his mercy? Granted that God could see him, but circumstances suggested—and the fact that so few books survive confirms—that God quite often had other things to worry about. It might therefore be the better form of wisdom to remind the reader at close quarters. A word of warning spoken in church might be dulled by time. A curse spoken might go half unheard, unheeded, or worse: an Arab, for instance, when he was cursed, would fling himself to the ground, knowing that the curse would thus pass over him and be gone.[16] A curse on the library door-post might go unseen; and a curse high on a wall when a man was looking down at a book? No, for an anathema to be effective—and its real purpose was as a preventive— it needed to be at the scene of the potential crime as an inescapable and unavoidable reminder. Hence the most popular form of the anathema, and the one described in the following pages—the anathema usually written at the end,* or inserted in the first page, or attached to the inside cover of a manuscript. This is the anathema in its purest form.

The anathemas were as diverse as the books. While all were inspired by the same heartfelt concern, the details of each curse depended on the particular circumstances and the creativity of the writer. In

---

*Not the last place a reader would look, but the first: in medieval times a work's title was stated at the end. Title pages were an invention of the latter part of the 15th century.

their own way the anathemas each reveal a bit of the inner-most feelings of the scribe and his ability to express them. For a good curse, like a good quiche, is an art to be savored.

If the earliest anathemas were short and simple and then, as time progressed, became more volatile and vituperative, they would best be displayed chronologically. But they meander from brief to bellicose with no respect for time and place. No scribe, of course, sat cursing in a vacuum. It was implicit in his craft that he copy the works of others, and therefore he could not help but come across the anathemas of other scribes, not only his contemporaries but as much as 1,000 years before his time. It would be reasonable to believe that he borrowed from and was influenced by others. In fact many anathemas appear virtually unchanged from century to century. But so many were lost with the destruction of their volumes, and so few of their authors have left more than their anathemas to mark their passing, that a serious "cultural" history of the anathema is impossible.

So I have arranged them in order of progressive complexity, for no other reason than that one has a natural tendency to want to bring order out of chaos, even if the chaos in this case is unrelated bits of invective. And I have saved for last the anathema I find the most clever, because it incorporated an element ignored by all the others—the visual.

Let us begin with some that are entirely gentle and nonthreatening and should not be considered curses at all, until one realizes that they lay on the reader a sense of responsibility—no, a sense of guilt, which everyone knows can be a curse in itself. Who would possibly, for example, be heartless enough to steal a book from a sweet thing like Miss Eleanor Worcester, when she had written, in 1440,

> This boke ys myne, Eleanor Worcester,
> And I yt los, and yow yt fynd,
> I pray yow hartely to be so kynd,
> That yow wel take a letil payne,
> To se my boke brothe home agayne.
> *London, British Museum,*
> *Ms. Harley 1,251, leaf 184*[107]

One can only assume that it was an effective tool, because it became popular not only in that century but later:

> An I it lose and you it find
> I pray you heartily to be so kind
> That you will take a little pain
> To see my book brought home again.[17]

In the same gentle vein—one book-lover appealing to the sense of cameraderie only another book-lover would fully understand—a mid-10th-century monk named Cild escalated the sentiment:

> Bald has this book which he told Cild to write
> In Christ's name all around I fondly pray
> That no foul fellow takes my book away
> By force or theft or any lying plight
> Why? For no treasure is so dear to me
> As those dear books Christ's grace accompanies.[31, 87]

> *Bald habet hunc librum Cild quem conscribere iussit.*
> *Hic precor assidue cunctis in nomine Christi,*
> *Quod nullus tollat hunc librum perfidus a me,*

Nec vi nec furto nec quodam famine falso.
Cur? Quia nulla mihi tam cara est optima gaza
Quam cari libri quos Christi gratia comit.

Another approach was that of sparing a fellow book-lover unnecessary pain:

If this book of mine be defiled with dirt, the master will smite me in dire wrath upon the hinder parts.[17]

To the wish for physical well-being add the irresistible suggestion that only a smart reader could be expected to be considerate of the book—and we have an even more powerful presentation. A scribe wrote in the 12th century:

This book, o Christ, in praise of thee,
Lies finished for all to see.
Good Benedictine, to spare my health,
Put back this book upon its shelf;
And you will give me recompense
If you deem it worthy of your intelligence.

Quem pro te, Christe, scripsi,
Liber explicit iste.
Hunc, Benedicte bone,
Mihi conservando repone,
Tuque recompenses,
Dignum si quomodo censes.
                    Cod. Lat. Monac. 4514[15]

liber sce marie de colūba. qcūq; eū furat' fuerit. uel alienauerit. Anathema Sit. Amen.

Plate 18: *A CISTERCIAN'S SIMPLE CURSE. Most book curses commonly were precise and to the point, it being necessary only to stipulate excommunication and leave the rest to the miscreant's imagination. A scribe in the Cistercian Monastery of Santa Maria della Colomba in the diocese of Piacenza, Italy, completing a manuscript in the late 12th century, stated cause and effect in as matter-of-fact a manner possible. (Courtesy of Mr. H. Clifford Maggs, Maggs Bros. Ltd., London)*

But enough of all these niceties. Reality suggests that when it comes to the way people can treat books, a plea aimed at the reader's sense of gentility and compassion isn't worth the ink wasted on it. Conscience is one thing, a good curse quite another.

The simplest anathema is no more than a reminder, the thought being, perhaps, that the imagination can suggest greater horrors than the pen. With that in mind, many scribes got directly to the point. A 12th-century Cistercian monk in the Monastery of Santa Maria della Colomba (near Piacenza, Italy) jotted in their copy of Pope Gregory's *Homiliae super Evangelia*[52] (Plate 18):

Book of Santa Maria della Colomba {literally, Holy Mother of the Dove}. Whoever steals it or sells it, may there be anathema on him. Amen.*[38]

Liber sancte marie de columba. quicumque eum furatus fuerit. uel alienauerit. Anathema. Sit. Amen.

Minimal maledictions—at least in terms of length—were similarly popular in many manuscripts of St. Alban's Monastery:

*The use of the Hebrew word "amen" meaning *truly* or any sign of agreement seems to have arisen when early Greek and Latin scholars produced copies of the *New Testament*. They inserted the Hebrew word at the end of passages they found especially moving.[30]

> This book belongs to S. Alban. May whosoever steals it from him or destroys its title be anathema. Amen.¹³
>
> *Hic est liber sancti Albani quem qui ei abstulerit aut titulum deleverit anathema sit. Amen.*

Adding a bit in length in order to get in some credits along with the curse, an early 9th-century scribe in the scriptorium of the Monastery of Lyons wrote

> This book is dedicated at the altar of Saint Stephen in accordance with the vow of Remigius, the humble bishop; may grace be to the reader, indulgence to the benefactor, anathema upon its thief.
>
> *Liber oblatus ad altare sancti Stephani ex voto Remigii humilis episcopi; Sit utenti gratia, largitori venia, fraudanti anathema.*
> Jerome on Isaiah
> Ms. Lyons 463(392) folio 171

And since anathema was, in effect, a weapon, another scribe combined that thought with the curse's terminal potential, and wrote

> May the sword of anathema slay
> If anyone steals this book away.¹⁰¹
>
> *Si quis furetur,*
> *anathematis ense necetur.*

Two other terse threats are interesting because their scribes were either fed to the cowl with their mistakes being pointed out, or tired of having to defend their manuscripts' literary content. Whatever the reason, both decided that since they were in full curse anyway, they might as well cover whatever else bothered them:

> If anyone steal it, let him be anathema!
> Whoever finds fault with it, let him be accursed. Amen.
>
> *Quicunque alienaverit anathema sit.*
> *Qui culpat carmen sit maledictus. Amen.*
>   Paraphrase of the Psalms,
>   Oxford, Bodleian Library[43]

And by a scribe in 1270:

> If anyone unfairly
> This scribe puts down,
> In Hell's murky waters
> May Cerberus him drown.*[15]
>
> *Scriptorem si quis verbis*
> *reprobarit iniquis,*
> *Cerberus in baratro*
> *flumine mergat atro.*

Occasionally the term "anathema" (whether specifying excommunication or simply a curse in general) does not appear at all. But the threat of excommunication is no less clear. The Greek Patriarch Athanasius (late 13th–early 14th centuries) wrote the following, in Arabic, at the bottom of the first page of *Genesis* of the Bible he

---

*Cerberus was the three-headed dog who guarded the gates of Hell. There is more to this anathema, but only the lines protecting the scribe are quoted, not the lines protecting the book.

held in his care, the 5th- or 6th-century *Codex Alexandrinus*, one of the three oldest, surviving, complete Greek Bibles:[86]

> Whoever shall remove it thence {from the cell of the Patriarch of Alexandria} shall be accursed and cut off. Written by Athanasius the humble.*

The allusion to being *cut off* quite likely meant separated from the Church body, i.e., excommunicated. A similar allusion is that of the *Book of Life* which, in Biblical language, was the volume in which were recorded the names of all those who merited Eternal Life.[64] If you couldn't be "found in the book," your future was eternal damnation. Hence, in the 7th or 8th century,

> He who erases the memory {of the fact that the book was bought by the monastery}, his name will be erased in the Book of Life.
> *Manuscript, British Museum*
> *Syrian Manuscript Nitrian collection.*[15]

And in the 16th century, in a missal belonging to Robert at Jumieges, France, is found

> Should anyone by craft or any device whatever abstract this book from this place may his soul suffer, in retribution for what he has done, and may his name be erased from the book of the living and not be recorded among the Blessed.[23]

*Apparently immune to his own curse, Athanasius later took the Bible with him when he moved to Constantinople.

These examples are sufficient to illustrate anathemas whose impact depended upon the reader's imagination. Scribes were certainly willing to enlarge upon the unpleasant eventualities. One way was to get a lot of people behind the curse. A trio of book producers in 1215 decided that at least a dozen were called for:

> This sacred gospel has been copied by the hand of George, priest of Rhodes, by the exertions and care of Athanasius, cloistered monk, and by the labour of Christonymus Chartinos, for their souls' health. If any man dare carry it off, either secretly or publicly, let him incur the malediction of the twelve apostles and let him also receive the heavier curse of all monks. Amen. The first day of the month of September, year 6743, of Jesus Christ 1215.[59]

Apostles provided a powerful element, and throwing in all the monks from *everywhere* was a nice touch, so George does deserve credit. But he only mentioned in passing a single source of curses far more weighty than any number elsewhere: God or Christ. Other scribes saw no need for anything else:

> Christ's curse upon the crook
> Who takes away this book.*[38, 96]
>
> *Sit maledictuus per Christum,*
> *Qui librum subtraxerit istum.*

A similar anathema:

---

*Medieval Latin resists translation; words or phrases changed in meaning due to their position or even the decade in which they were penned. To convey medieval Latin rhyme into its English equivalent takes a special talent, so I am grateful to a friend for some examples in this chapter:

I bow in thanks to David Harvey,
Who finds it fun to fashion rhyme.
It's simply play where he's concerned;
I know its not where I'm.

> Thys boke is one
> and Godes kors ys anoder;
> They take the ton,
> God gefe them the toder.[101]

Or more clearly, in a manuscript of the 15th century,

> This book is one,
> And God's curse is another;
> They that take the one
> God give them the other.[17]

An improvement emphasized the severity of the curse by pointing out its duration:

> Whosoever removes this Volume from this same mentioned Convent, may the anger of the Lord overtake him in this world and in the next to all eternity. Amen.[29]

In the mid-11th century, Bishop Leofric of Exeter was in charge of the Library of Exeter Cathedral and was responsible for anathemas appearing in many of the books. One that best represents them (Plate 19) reads

> Leofric, Bishop of the Church of St. Peter the Apostle in Exeter, gives this book to his cathedral church, for the relief of his soul and for the use of his successors. If, however, anyone shall take it away from thence, let him lie under perpetual malediction. Amen.

Plate 19: A BISHOP'S BOOK CURSE. When Bishop Leofric of Exeter presented a volume to his cathedral, it was a boon of such value that he had no intention of its ever being moved elsewhere. The cost, he made quite clear, was eternal damnation. (Oxford, Bodleian Library, Ms. Auct. F 3.6, folio 111 verso)

Hunc librum dat leofricus episcopus ecclesiae Sancti Petri Apostoli in exonia ad sedem suam episcopalem, pro remedio animae suae, ad utilitatem successorum suorum. Siquis autem illum inde abstulerit, perpetuae maledictioni subiaceat. fiat.

                Oxford, Bodleian Library, in a copy of the Prudentius. (Ms. Auct. F3.6, folio III verso)[5, 38]

And from the Monastery of St. Emmeram,

> If anyone takes this book from Emmeram without permission, may he fear the judgment of the Lord. Whoever takes this book and does not afterward return it in good condition, may he do penance forever as his just reward.[101]

    Hemrammo librum si quis vi subtrahat istum,
    Juditium Domini sibimet sciat esse timori.
    Quisquis percipiat quod non bene postea reddat,
    Hic capiat munus quod semper sit luiturus.

Since God, when all is said and done, is an intangible, a little direct reference to physical violence added spice to a curse. One way was to suggest it in a general fashion:

    Who takes this book from holy St. Nazarius
    The Judge's wrath will make his life precarious.[31]

    Hoc qui Nazarium libro fraudaverit almum
    Sentiat ultricem districti iudicis iram.

Or

> May whoever steals me cease
> Ever to have a moment's peace.[101]
>
> *Qui me furetur,*
> *nunquam requies sibi detur.*

Something definitely could be said for pinpointing just how uncomfortable things could get. From a copy of Chaucer's *Troilus:*

> He that thys Boke rentt or stelle
> God send hym sekenysse swart of helle.[80]

Plate 20: THE CURATOR'S BOOK CURSE. While most book curses attracted attention by dint of their content rather than their appearance, being simply penned amid if not following the final few lines of a manuscript, one might infrequently be found that was as glorious to see as it was aggressive to contemplate. Perhtolt, curator of the Abbey of St. Peter in Salzburg, Austria, while promising intense physical agony to miscreants, had the good taste to do so in pure gold on precious purple. It may have been only the 11th century, but the medium, if it wasn't the message, could at least make the message very noticeable. (New York, The Pierpont Morgan Library, M. 780, folio 80)

No, *sekenysse* won't quite do; a lot of things that make you *seke* can't be guaranteed to leave you in agony, even though the idea that it would be "just short of Hell" does have rather a panache. But scribes certainly could be called upon to be a bit more bloodthirsty in a good cause. Perhtolt, at the Abbey of St. Peter in Salzburg, Austria, in the latter half of the 11th century, not only had the right idea, but expressed it in gold letters (see Plate 20) on the last purple-stained vellum page of a lectionary he was completing:

> To the bearer of the keys of Heaven {St. Peter, patron of Perhtolt's monastery} the Curator Perhtolt who made this book offers it with joyful heart in order that it may be an expiation for all sins committed by him. May he who steals it suffer violent bodily pains.
> COELI CLAVIGERO DONAVIT LAETO CUSTOS HUNC LIBRUM PERHTOLT QUI FECERIT ILLUMVT SIT PECCATI PRECIVM. PER CVNCTA PATRATI HINC RAPTOR POENAS
> *New York, Pierpont Morgan Library,*
> *M. 780, folio 80*[10, 82]

And equally to the point, in the 13th century,

> May he who steals you then be sent
> A blow upon his fundament.[101]
>
> *Qui te furetur,*
> *in culum percutietur.*

And, undated,

> Who steals me, rightily
> Hit with a rod, mightily.[15]
>
> *Qui me furetur,*
> *baculo bene percutietur.*

From the year 1461:

> Hanging will do
> for him who steals you.[15]
>
> *Qui me furatur,*
> *in tribus tignis suspendatur.*

A 14th-century scribe who couldn't decide between bisection or banishment simply included both:

> May the one who takes you in theft
> By the sword of a demon be cleft.
> May he for one full year be banned
> Who tries to take you away in hand.[101]
>
> *Qui te furetur*
> *hic demonis ense secetur.*
> *Iste sit in banno*
> *qui te furetur in anno.*

Hugh, the abbot of the Abbey of Lobbes in Germany, was apparently having "one of those days" in 1049, as he sat finishing the compilation of a library catalogue.⁹³ Apparently a number of the monastery's books were missing, or at least he was having quite a time getting the borrowers to return them, for he wrote on the last page

> All those who do not books return
> Are thieves, not borrowers, and earn
> The punishment Justice demands;
> Their sacrificial loss of hands.
> May God, therefore, as witness see
> That it be done unswervingly.⁹³
>
> *Omnis librorum*
> *raptor nec redditor horum*
> *Penas suscipiat*
> *et manibus hostia fiat.*
> *Sit justus vindex*
> *raptus recti deus index.*

Nasty, certainly, but a fine bit of simplistic justice; for it is the hands that take a book away. Why? So that the eyes can read the book. Hence the obvious emphasis in this next, ever more eviscerating example (Plate 21):

> The finished book before you lies;
> This humble scribe don't criticize.
> Whoever takes away this book
> May he never on Christ look.
> Whoever to steal this volume durst

ANATHEMA! 77

Plate 21: AN EVISCERATING BOOK CURSE. *Book curses were a confusing amalgam of repetition of the familiar format, thoughtful concern, and less than rational emotionalism. Since the degree of each varied with the individual scribe, the variety was endless and always curious. A 13th-century scribe who began his explicit with gentle humility warmed up rapidly as he got to cursing. Instead of escalating the level of his threats, his concern for his book led him first to damnation, then murder, and finally to a rather anti-climactic evisceration.* (Rome, Vatican Library, Vatic. Palat. Lat. 978, folio 25 recto, col. 2)

May he be killed as one accursed.
Whoever to steal this volume tries
Out with his eyes, out with his eyes![38]

Explicit iste liber
sit scriptor crimine liber.
Non videat Christum
qui librum subtrahet istum.
Hunc qui furetur
anathematis esse necetur
Ut me furetur
qui nitatur exoculetur.
    13th century (?), Rome, Vatican Library,
    Ms. Palat. Lat. 978, folio 25r, col. 2[96]

 An anonymous scribe, probably in Germany, made a significantly gory improvement to the latter thought by adding detail, sound effects, *and* justification. The Grand Guignol school of poetic expression employed by this scribe is a bit misleading; he obviously had a good sense of humor, for each line begins in Latin and ends in German:

This book belongs to none but me
For there's my name inside to see.
To steal this book, if you should try,
It's by the throat that you'll hang high.
And ravens then will gather 'bout
To find your eyes and pull them out.
And when you're screaming "oh, oh, oh!"
Remember, you deserved this woe.[80]

Hic liber est mein
Ideo nomen scripsi drein.
Si vis hunc liberum stehlen,
Pendebis an der kehlen.
Tunc veniunt die raben
Et volunt tibi oculos ausgraben.
Tunc clamabis ach ach ach,
Ubique tibi recte geschach.

Modern psychology stresses that negotiation is impossible when one party puts another in an inflexible position; matters can always be worked out if alternatives are offered. And this was not lost on the medieval scribe. We have seen him, in earlier anathemas, offer to lift the curse if the book is returned, but we were concerned at the time with other ingredients in those quotes. But the inclusion of mitigating circumstances was popular (see Plate 22):

This book belongs to Christ Church, Canterbury, from the gift of Master John Blund (Chancellor of York). The contents of the volume are as follows, namely these books of the Apocrypha: Esdras (Nehemiah) Tobias Judith Esther and the Book of Maccabees; and may whoever destroys this title, or by gift or sale or loan or exchange or theft or by any other device knowingly alienates this book from the aforesaid Christ Church {Canterbury} incur in his life the malediction of Jesus Christ and of the most glorious Virgin His Mother, and of Blessed Thomas, Martyr. Should however it please Christ, who is patron of Christ Church, may his soul be saved in the Day of Judgment.

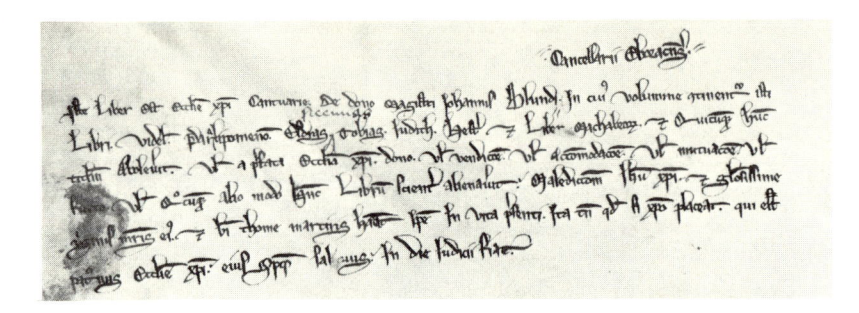

Iste liber est ecclesie Christi Cantuarie De dono Mag. Johannis Blundi (Cancellarii Eboracensis). In cuius volumine continentur isti libri, videlicet Paralipomenon Esdras (Neemias) Tobias Judith Hester et Liber Machabeorum et quicunque hunc titulum aboleuerit uel a prefata ecclesia Christi dono • uel uendicione • uel accommodacione • uel mutuacione • uel furto • uel quocunque alio modo hunc librum scienter alienauerit malediccionem Ihesu Christi et gloriosissime Virginis matris eius et beati thome martiris habeat ipse in uita presenti. Ita tamen quod si christo placeat • qui est patronus ecclesie Christi • eius spiritus saluus in die Judicii fiat.
                    Cambridge, Trinity College Library,
                    163, Libri Paralipomenon Etc. Glosati.
                    B.5.17 240, folio 192b.[13, 24, 38, 98]

Plate 22: THE CHRIST CHURCH BOOK CURSE. *Justice, mercy, and good will toward one's fellow man were ethics inseparable from the medieval religious mind. But it was not inconsistent that the same mind could happily contemplate the severest pain for a heinous crime—like stealing a book. Book curses occasionally followed the sanguinary course with the hope of salvation, as in this valued manuscript from the library of Christ Church, Canterbury. (Cambridge, Trinity College Library, 163, Libri Paralipomenon Etc. Glosati. B.5.17 240, folio 192b)*

Similarly, in a manuscript from the year 1067, with a common variation—that the thief can cause the absolution:

> Whoever takes this book or steals it or in some evil way removes it from the church of Saint Caecilia, may he be damned and cursed forever unless he returns it or atones for his act. So be it. So be it. Amen. Amen.[101]

> *Quicumque istum librum rapuerit aut furaverit vel aliquo malo ingenio abstulerit ab aecclesia S. Caeciliae sit perpetua damnatione damnatus et maledictus nisi reddiderit vel emendaverit. FIAT FIAT AMEN AMEN.*

Unlike his contemporaries, who were doomed but for atonement, the German malefactor had another means of escape—albeit an unlikely one. He would have been "spell-proof" at the time of the crime if he had had the foresight to be wearing, according to German folklore, a shirt both spun and stitched by a maiden who had not spoken a word for seven years.[16] It is quite likely there was a paucity of that sort of exceptional woman in Germany or elsewhere in that or any time, beyond the confines of a nunnery operated under the Rule of Silence.* And no thinking nun would have supplied the curse-shirking shirt, because nuns were equal to monks as fine calligraphers, book producers, and book-lovers.

Another ingredient that had appeared earlier in anathemas and not been given concentration worthy of its impact was Hell. To medieval minds, Hell was not a concept but a vivid reality, more easily reached and more anxious to accept him than we can truly understand today. A good anathema was even better with a bit of nether geography suggested. Readers leafing through Rufinus Tyrannius's translation of Origen's *De Principiis* knew precisely what real

---

*A nunnery always housed women. A convent could house men or women or both; only in modern times has "convent" been taken to mean "for women only."

estate he was referring to when he threatened tamperers with damnation in

> the place where there is wailing and gnashing of teeth and where the fire never goes out.[95]

But most scribes simply spelled it out, like this 9th-century scribe from Lorsch:

> Whoe'er this book / To make his own doth plot,
> The fires of Hell / and brimstone be his lot.[24]

And in the words of brother Ruotpertus, fatigued from copying the *Echternach Bible*,

> The Holy abbot Reginbertus is the author of this book and the scribe is brother Ruotpertus. In this book let their lives be recorded and be remembered forever. If anyone takes this book from Saint Willibrodus or those serving him, may he be consigned to the depths of hell and may he be accursed. So be it. So be it. Amen.[15]
>
> *Dominus abbas Reginbertus auctor libri huius et frater Ruotpertus scriptor. In libro vitae scribantur et in memoria eterna habeantur. Si quis hunc librum sancto Willibrodo illique servientibus abstulerit, tradatur diabolo et omnibus infernalibus penis et sit anathema. fiat. fiat. amen.*

While we're here in the depths we ought to acknowledge the rather

uncreative but certainly articulate literary school founded on the
theory that the most direct way to increase impact is to say it all
over again. A master of this school of *dejà vu* was a 9th-century
scribe from Lorsch, who wrote in the *Codex Pithoeanus of Juvenal and
Persius*:

> The book of Saint Nazarius Martyr of Christ.
> Whoever wishes to appropriate this book of mine for himself,
> may he endure the fire and brimstone of hell.
> Whoever wishes to appropriate this book of mine for himself,
> May he endure the fire and brimstone of hell.[23]
>
> > *Codex Sancti Nazarii Martiris Christi.*
> > *Qui cupit hunc librum sibimet contendere privum,*
> > *Hic Flegetonteas patiatur sulphure flammas.*
> > *Qui cupit hunc librum sibimet contendere privum,*
> > *Hic Flegetonteas patiatur sulphure flammas.*

A more-sophisticated way to escalate the impact of Hell is to place
it in context as the opposite of Heaven:

> > May he who wrote this book with his pen
> > Ascend to Heaven full well;
> > If anyone takes it away again
> > May his soul rot away in Hell.[38, 96]
> >
> > *Libri contractor calamis celi potiatur;*
> > *Si quis subtractor, in Avernis sic moriatur.*

Another way to emphasize Hell's disadvantages is to point out whose companionship one would lose if sent there:

> May no one take way this book from here throughout the whole of time, if he desires to have a share with Gallus.*
>
> *Auferat hunc librum nullus hinc omne per aevum*
> *Cum Gallo partem quisquis habere cupit.*
> From a manuscript in the library of the
Monastery of St. Gall[54, 71]

*I.e., to retire to Heaven with the founder of the monastery.

On the other hand, Hell might well seem far worse if one were reminded of who was waiting there to be one's eternal next-door neighbor. Walter the Priest was on to a good thing late in the 12th century in Austria (see Plate 23) when he wrote

> The book of Walter the Priest. May whoever steals it be accursed. Amen. May the earth that swallowed up Datan and Abiron engulf him, and may he share the lot of Judas in hell.†
>
> *Liber Sacerdotis Walteri Siquis ei abstulerit anathema sit. amen absorbeat eum terra que d'glutiuit datan & abiron & parte jude recipiat in inferno.*
> St. Gregory's *Expositio Novi Testamenti*,
Cambridge, Harvard College Library,
Ms. Typ 205H[88]

†Dathan and Abiram conspired together and rebelled against Moses (see *Numbers* 16).[1]

And even more neighbors,

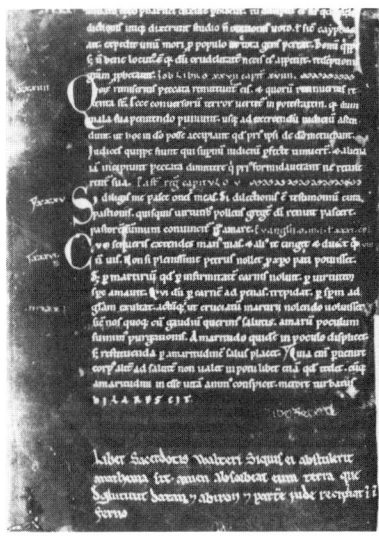

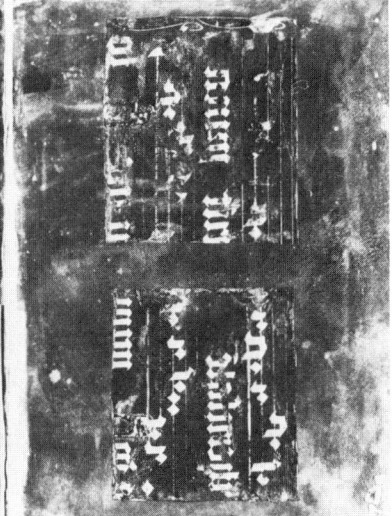

ANATHEMA! 85

Plate 23: THE PRIEST'S BOOK CURSE. *Some book curses were not particularly creative, but should be given credit for covering a lot of territory. The 12th-century Austrian priest Walter, in few words and directly to the point, managed to refer both to the here and the hereafter, establish associations both with the Old and New Testaments, claim ownership to the volume, suggest his familiarity with religious history, and expect no less than that acquaintance from the reader. (Cambridge, Harvard College Library, Ms. Typ 205H)*

So that if anyone by any means takes it away from the monastery with no intention of returning it, may he receive the fate of eternal damnation with Judas the traitor, and Anna, and Caiaphas.* Amen, amen. So be it, so be it.[54]

Ut si quis eum de monasterio aliquo ingenio non redditurus abstraxerit, cum Juda proditore, Anna, et Caiapha, portionem aeternae damnationis accipiat. Amen, amen. Fiat, fiat.

*A bad neighborhood indeed: Caiaphas was the high priest before whom Jesus stood trial (see *Matthew* 26:3, *Luke* 3:2, and *John* 18:13). If the scribe meant to write Annas, the reference was to Caiaphas's father-in-law, the Jewish high priest (see *John* 18:13); or if Ananias, he meant the disciple who tried to deceive the Church (see *Acts* 5) or the high priest who laid charges against Paul (see *Acts* 23:2, 24:1).[2]

And from a Benedictine monastery in France,

> This book belongs to S. Maximin at his monastery of Micy, which abbat Peter caused to be written, and with his own labor corrected and punctuated, and on Holy Thursday dedicated to God and S. Maximin on the altar of St. Stephen, with this imprecation that he who should take it away from thence by what device soever, with the intention of not restoring it, should incur damnation with the traitor Judas, with Annas, Caiaphas, and Pilate. Amen.[23]

Close as Hell might be, the anathema could promise a hell even closer—a hell on earth, or excommunication. A popular medieval anathema was

> May whoever steals or alienates this book, or mutilates it, be cut off from the body of the church and held as a thing accursed, an object of loathing.[24]

And there were fine distinctions, too, in the *degree* of excommunication. Lesser excommunication meant exclusion from the Sacraments. Greater excommunication meant being cut off from *all* contact with the Church.[38] Hence this 13th-century English anathema (Plate 24):

> This is the book of St. James of Wigmore. If anyone takes it away or maliciously destroys this notice in taking it away from the above-mentioned place, may he be tied by the chain of greater excommunication. Amen. So be it. So be it. So be it.

Hic est liber S. Jacobi de Wygemora • si quis eum alienaurerit vel titulum hunc malitiose deleuerit a dicto loco alienando uinculo excommunicationis maioris innodetur • amen • fiat • fiat • fiat •
   Cambridge, Trinity College Library,
   B.2.23 290, folio 1[38, 98]

Thus the meaning of the "great Sentence" mentioned in the Breviary in the library of Gonville and Caius College, Cambridge:

> Where so ever y be come over all
> I belonge to the Chapell of Gunvylle hall;
> He shall be cursed by the grate-sentens
> That felonsly faryth and berith me thens.
> And whether he bere me in pooke or sekke,
> For me he shall be hanged by the nekke,
> (I am so well beknown of dyverse men)
> But I be restored theder again.[95]

As we have seen, when it came to anathemas, some were brief and some wordy, some mild and some imaginative; but the less they left to the mind's eye, the more threatening they became. The best threat is the one that really lets you know, in specific detail, what physical anguish is all about. The more creative the scribe, the more delicate the detail, as in this quaint suggestion at the end of a Bible written and illuminated at the Premonstratensian abbey of Arnstein, near Coblenz (Plate 25).[84] The scribe, probably Brother Lunardus, wrote in 1172:[28]

Plate 24: THE ST. JAMES BOOK CURSE. If excommunication was, in the Middle Ages, the ultimate punishment for the greatest transgressions—book theft definitely included—it was not a simple blanket sentence. There were degrees of damnation and, in the case of a book in the English monastery of St. James of Wigmore in the 13th century, the prospect of the book—and even the curse—being tampered with merited the severest form. (Cambridge, Trinity College Library, B.2.23 290, folio 1)

Book of {the Abbey of} Saints Mary and Nicholas of Arnstein: If anyone take away this book, let him die the death; let him be fried in a pan; let the falling sickness and fever seize him; let him be broken on the wheel, and hanged. Amen.*

Liber sancte Marie sanctiq; Nycolai in Arinstein: quem si quis abstulerit, morte moriatur; in sartagine coquatur; caducus morbus instet eum et febres; et rotatur, et suspendatur. Amen.

London, British Museum, Ms. Harley 2798, folio 235 verso.²¹

Not specific enough? Then let us turn to the Monastery of San Pedro in Barcelona:

For him that stealeth, or borroweth and returneth not, this book from its owner, let it change into a serpent in his hand & rend him. Let him be struck with palsy, & all his members blasted. Let him languish in pain crying aloud for mercy, & let there be no surcease to his agony till he sing in dissolution. Let bookworms gnaw his entrails in token of the Worm that dieth not,† & when at last he goeth to his final punishment, let the flames of Hell consume him for ever.²⁴

Once we regain our composure, we notice the emphasis on unpleasant creatures dispensing ultimate discomforts. For some reason pigs, too, joined the ranks with a poor public image—at least as far as Simon Vostre of Paris was concerned in 1502. Completing a Book of Hours, he left no sty unturned in warning

ANATHEMA! 88

*In another source the translation of the same words reads "boiled in a cauldron" instead of "fried in a pan."⁴³ The actual meaning may well be either; I suggest one simply choose whichever is the more disquieting. The "falling sickness" is epilepsy. An ancient cure, recorded by Pliny, was to thrust a nail into the ground where the epileptic had fallen. The disease would be transferred to the nail and thence to the ground, leaving the victim free.⁷²

†One of the pains of Hell, mentioned in *Mark* and *Isaiah*, was to have one's soul devoured eternally by a worm (or serpent or dragon).⁶⁴

Whoever steals this Book of Prayer
May he be ripped apart by swine,
His heart be splintered, this I swear,
And his body dragged along the Rhine.

{Old French:}
Descire soit de truyes et porceaulx
Et puys son corps trayne en leaue du Rin
Le cueur fendu decoupe par morceaulx
Qui ces heures prendra par larcin.

{Modern French:}
Dechire soit de truies et pourceaux
Et puis son corps traine en l'eau du Rhin
Le coeur fendu decoupe par morceaux
Qui ces Heures prendra par larcin.

Paris, PML 18206,
inner upper cover[10, 38]

People have for ages known the value of responsive reading; draw the fellow in, make him part of it, and you make a stronger impression. Credit one scribe, therefore, near the end of the Middle Ages, with creating an anathema unique in its approach:

He that steals this booke
Shall be hanged on a hooke.
He that this book stelle wolde,
Sone be his herte colde.

Plate 25: THE TWO SAINTS' BOOK CURSE. *Surely anyone can curse, given the motivation—and book theft was certainly sufficient cause. But in the maelstrom of medieval maledictae one occasionally sees the work of a master. So credit should be given to Brother Lunardus who, c. 1172, to keep his book from being stolen from the Abbey of Sts. Mary and Nicholas, neatly combined death, boiling alive, epilepsy, fever, dismemberment, and strangulation without the least bit of maudlin sentimentality and in a directness of point and economy of wording. (London, The British Library, Ms. Harley 1798, folio 235 verso)*

>That it may so be,
>Seith Amen for charite.
>>*15th century(?)*[43]

Abbot Whethamstede of St. Albans considered hanging a punishment worth the crime. When a volume of Valerius Maximus was produced under his direction, he ordered the following anathema inserted:

>If anyone steals this book may he come to the gallows or the rope of Judas.
>>*Oxford, Bodleian Library,*
>>*Humphrey's Manuscript*[43]

I point it out because reference to the rope of Judas is rare (the previously mentioned anathema of Bernhard of Montfaulcon is the only other one I've found). And I wonder if the suggestion could be, since the rope apparently refers to Judas's suicide by hanging, a curse of being driven—by remorse—to suicide.

My favorite anathema intrigues me not for the words alone, but for the way in which the anonymous medieval scribe set it down. It appears thus:

>Sor   sup   no   scrip   li   poti
>   te   er   rum   tor   bri   atur
>Mor   inf   no   rap   li   mori[51]

which is an ingenious way of writing

> *Sorte supernorum scriptor libri potiatur*
> *Morte infernorum raptor libri moriatur*

In English, rhymed, it might be loosely arranged as

> May he who wrote this book procure the joys of life supernal;
> steals endure pangs death infernal.[38]

A curse laid today, for whatever good reason, can in some cases become a problem tomorrow. A book was often legitimately traded or sold. Along with it, neatly inscribed, went its anathema, and a problem for the new owner. In 1327 the Bishop of Exeter was confronted with this problem, hence the dual notations in a copy of the works of Augustine and Ambrose now in the Bodleian Library, Oxford University. First, the anathema:

> This book belongs to St. Mary of Robert's Bridge; whoever steals it, or sells it, or takes it away from this house in any way, or injures it, let him be anathema-maranatha.[54, 80]
>
> *Liber S. Mariae de Ponte Roberti,* qui eum abstulerit, aut vendiderit, vel quolibet modo ab hac domo alienaverit, vel quamlibet ejus partem abscideret, sit anathema maranatha. Amen.

And beneath it, John added as best he could:

> I, John, bishop of Exeter, do not know where the said house is: I did not steal this book, but got it lawfully.[54, 80]
>
> *Ego, Joannes, Exon Epus, nescio ubi est domus predicta, nec hunc librum abstuli, sed modo legitimo adquisivi.*

John's emphatic response may have been instigated by the particular nastiness of the anathema, for it threatened not just *anathema* but *anathema-maranatha*. It is appropriately a phrase "full of sound and fury, signifying nothing," as curse-acquainted Shakespeare put it. *Maranatha* is Aramaic for "Our Lord has come" or "O, our Lord, Come Thou" (see 1 *Corinthians* 16:22). It was believed by some that to combine it with *anathema*, as in *anathema-maranatha*, was to increase the potency enormously. Thus it becomes the highest degree of excommunication,[64] although what this might be is not explained—or too terrible to discuss? Its use is interesting because the vast proportion of medieval people were uneducated, so Latin was to many, because of its Church use, awe-inspiring. It was therefore not uncommon to accentuate something by adding a phrase in gibberish whose sound was similar to a Latin Church invocation, in order to make it more impressive.

Robert Colston faced an almost similar dilemma. The book he acquired contained, at its end:

> Ihesus marya.
> Mysterys felys* owyth thys boke:

*Mistress Phyllis?

and she yt lose, and you yt fynde,
I pray you to take the payne
to bryng my boke home agayne.
Ihesus maria.[17]
>   *London, British Museum,*
>   *Ms. Eg. 1,151, leaf 159*

It wasn't really a curse (short of the implied responsibility), but the suggestion might remain that he'd stolen it; so Robert felt called upon to set the record straight. Uncursed, he felt in light enough mood to have fun with the situation, and therefore created a bilingual rhyming response:

> *Iste liber attinet* {this book belongs},
>   deny it if you can,
> *Ad me* {to me}, *Robbertum Colston,*
>   a very honest man.[17]

Earlier in this chapter I mentioned that the first, or rather the oldest-known, anathema that specifically refers to excommunication—the curse that gave anathema its name—was created in 627. I had a reason for not quoting it: I mentioned that anathema did not follow a particular evolution, but varied in length, cleverness, and aggression dependent solely upon the scribe's interest, ability, and familiarity with the vituperation of his contemporaries and those who had preceded him for many centuries. To find a logical course through this chaos of curses I arbitrarily chose to introduce first the simplest and then those involving specific additional elements—God,

Christ, Hell, physical pain, disease, extended durations, biblical references, posterity, recourse to absolution, etc.—and then combinations of two or more of the above.

It is ironic that the earliest known truly "anathematic" anathema contains every one of the above elements. To quote it now brings us conveniently full circle. To have quoted it earlier would have, in a manner of speaking, brought us to the end just as we were about to begin.

The curse was apparently called for because in 627 a book was given to the Abbey of St.-Denis.[95] Whether it was because the donor was so important, the book so valuable, or the act so surprising, we no longer know; but something caused the scribe to ascend into such florid, exuberant, formal Latin, in such compound and complex phraseology, that no one in the intervening 1,356 years has apparently succeeded in translating what the scribe thought he was writing. At the same time it is inconceivable to suffer the loss of the seminal anathema simply because it is archaic gibberish. It certainly wasn't to him. So the problem was approached as an archaeologist might a trash-bin of disassociated pottery pieces: all the individual shards (or phrases) were gathered together and then, with the knowledge of the shape of different pots (or different curses) being known, the pieces were moved here and there until they formed a recognizable whole. As a result,* I believe it is safe to assume that the classic in this field (overlooking the cracks and holes) reads as follows:

> Therefore I entreat . . . God and the Angels and . . . every nation of mankind, whether near or far, that no hindrance presumes against my

---

*It would have been impossible to put the curse back together had not Michael W. O'Laughlin been so interested and expert in putting the pieces into English and helping me position them.

work. If {anyone} acts against my work with his hands, would that the Eternal King {take} this cursed person and lower {him} into the lowest level of Hell {to be} tortured with Judas, and anathema and maranatha. {Let him also receive} by the hand of God the cruellest plague {and both he and his} sons struck with leprosy so that no one inhabit his house. {However, if he pays} double the value of {this work} in money, let him be absolved.[15]

Propterea rogo et contestor coram Deo et Angelis eius et omni natione hominum tam propinquis quam extraneis, ut nullus contra deliberationem meam impedimentum S. Dionysio de hac re facere praesumat; si fuerit, quia manus suas ad hoc apposuerit faciendo, aeternus rex peccata mea absolvat et ille maledictus in inferno inferiori et anathema et Maranatha percussus cum Juda cruciandis descendat, et peccatum quem amittit in filios et in domo sua crudelissime plaga ut leprose pro huius culpa a Deo percussus, ut non sit qui inhabitet in Domo eius, ut eorum plaga in multis timorem concutiat, et quantum res ipsa meliorata valuerit, duplex satisfactione fisco egenti exsolvat.

This curious history could, but doesn't, end here. For we have left John, the Bishop of Exeter, the uncomfortable object of a curse he didn't incur. It shouldn't be our intention to take advantage of his predicament, but his situation does open another vituperative vista for anathemas.

John was faced with the fact that the anathema was—or better yet was part of—a statement of ownership. A title was backed by a threat. It should not be surprising, then, that scribes who worked on books and were also employed in copying documents should see the advantage in protecting a charter or title with an anathema, just as they had a book. Such anathemas do exist, and I include a few here because they are also fine examples of naked aggression. From a Cartulary of the Monastery of St. Pere I in 1053:

> If anyone tries to diminish my gift or to lessen anything at all in this undertaking, may he be struck with the curse of Ham who in derision pointed out the naked body of his father to his brothers and may he also along with Dathan and Abiron whom the earth swallowed up alive and with Judas the betrayer who hanged himself and with Nero who crucified Peter and beheaded Paul. Unless he comes to his senses and make amends, may he suffer punishment in hell with the devil...[15]
>
> *Si quis autem huic largitioni meae contraire aut minuere ex hac re quippiam temptaverit, maledictione Cham, qui patris pudenda deridenda fratribus ostendit, feriatur, et cum Dathan et Abiron, quos terra vivos absorbuit, et cum Juda traditore, qui se suspendit laqueo, et cum Nerone, qui Petrum in cruce suspendit et Paullum decollavit, nisi resipuerit et ad satisfactionibus remedium confugerit, cum diabolo in inferno poenas luat ...*

In fact, it continues in such mounting antagonism that it cannot be translated coherently.

Eighty-four years later, in a Charter from King Stephen to the Priory of Eye in Suffolk, the hostility is tempered by the soothing *clink* of coin of the realm:[85]

> Whoever intentionally proposes to remove, or weaken, or thwart anything contained in this charter, let him be excommunicated, anathematized, and secluded from the fellowship of God and the portals of Holy Church by the power of Almighty God, Father, Son, and Holy

Spirit, and the Holy Apostles, and all the Saints until he shall pay out thirty pounds of gold to the royal authority. Let it be so. Amen, amen, amen.[25, 28]

Quicumque aliquid de his quae in hac carta continentur auferre, aut minuere, aut disturbare, scienter voluerit, auctoritate dei omnipotentis patris et filii et spiritus sancti, et sanctorum apostolorum et omnium sanctorum sit excommunicatus, anatematizatus, et a consortio dei et liminibus sanctae ecclesiae sequestratus donec resi piscat, et regi(a)e potestati xxx (triginta) libras auri persolvat. Fiat, Fiat, Fiat. Amen, Amen, Amen.*

The third and last I was able to find is rather special because it damns not only the transgressor, but his entire family down to and including his great-great-great-great-great-grandchildren. And should that not give him pause for thought, the curse proceeded down the family line, wiping out descendants generation by generation in *exponential progression* per each additional transgression (see Plate 26). Petrus Veremudi may have had good reason for his remarkable vehemence against anyone tampering with the grant he was writing in 1226 in Andradi, Spain. His sizable estate included all his property around the Church of St. Eulalia at Bureganes, and more near the Church of St. Martinus at Porto, and more near Monte Nigro, as well as additional land *and* other inheritances.[52] Petrus himself had once been up to no good, so *much* unspecified no good in fact, specifically in the Monastery of St. John of Calvary, that he seriously doubted where his soul would repose after his death. He was so uncertain, that rather than leave his large estate to his family, he thought it advisable to give it to the monastery—on condition that

---

*I am indebted to Sr. Wilma Fitzgerald and Prof. Paul Dutton of the Pontifical Institute of Mediaeval Studies, Toronto, for this house transcription, which they made directly from a photograph of the Charter (Plate V, Sotheby Phillippica V), and for the English translation appearing on an earlier page of this book. The Latin text differs from that published in Dugdale's *Monasticon Anglicanum* because, I am informed, Dugdale's version was taken from a Cartulary containing a copy of this Charter, and errors crept in along the way.

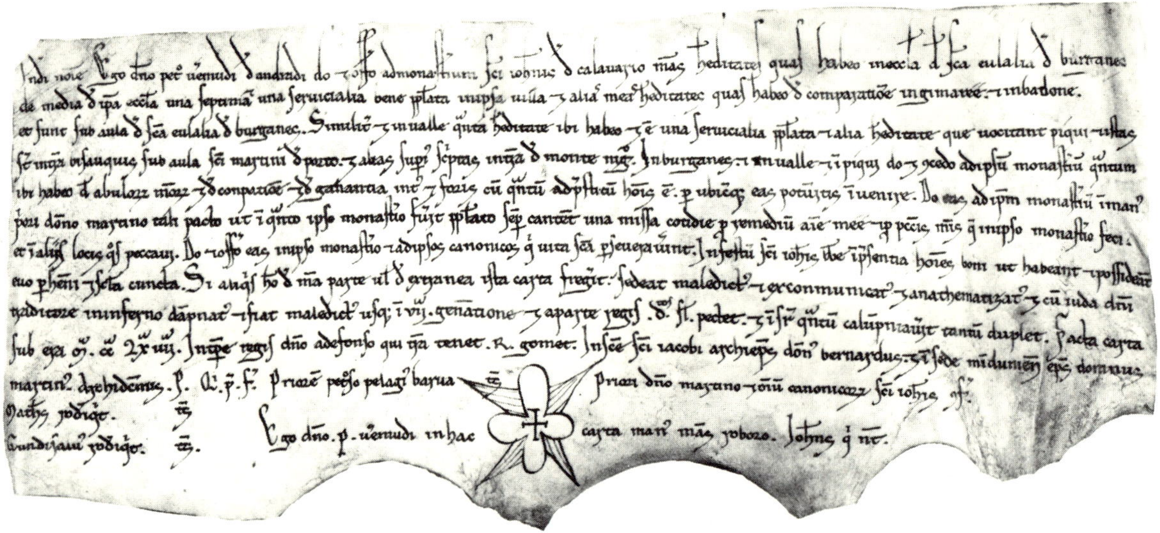

Plate 26: THE CHARTER CURSE. *The scribe who devoted himself to books would nonetheless occasionally find his hand for hire in accounting, copying wills and deeds, and writing letters dictated to him by an illiterate clientele. If a book were valuable and merited the protection of a curse, then a will, grant, or deed deserved no less, for it too could be stolen or—perhaps worse—altered to suit the perpetrator. Hence the inclusion in this Spanish charter of 1226 of a curse so clever that it could increase its power twofold forever. (Courtesy of Mr. H. Clifford Maggs, Maggs Bros. Ltd., London)*

the monks hold a mass *every day* for his soul. Since his misdeeds left his forwarding address in great doubt, the daily mass might make all the difference, and he strongly suspected that someone in his family, more interested in real estate than his resting place, could easily land him in Hell by contesting the grant. So he had good reason to stipulate that

> If any one of my lineage or anyone extraneous should violate this document, may curse and malediction and excommunication befall him, and may he be damned in Hell like Judas who betrayed the Lord, and may he be accursed unto the seventh generation; and in behalf of the King may he pay for it in like manner with the addition that inasmuch he deals fraudulently so many times (the curses) may be doubled.[52]

While the use of anathemas may have slowed with the advent of printing in the mid-15th century, it did not cease. There was no precedent for the printed book other than the handwritten one, so all the facets of the handwritten manuscript—from anathema to explicit, the lack of a title page, and the absence of page numbers—became the norm. Almost a century and a half after the arrival of printing, anathemas are recorded. One in particular was an anathema with a vengeance. Pope Sixtus V (1585–1590) issued a Papal Bull that promised automatic excommunication to any printer who might alter the text of the Vulgate Bible he had authorized to be printed. For good measure he ordered the printers to set the anathema in type at the beginning of the Bible. When the Bible was published, however, it contained so many errors that, when an attempt to save it by pasting in corrections failed, the edition was destroyed. Disconcerting as this may have been to Sixtus, it is even more so to the generally held belief that the closer one is to God, the more efficacious one's anathematic ferocity. The belief spanned cultures: the *Talmud* held that a scholar's (hence a student of God's word) curse was incapable of failure. The dying curse of a wizard or priest cast the greatest dread in the hearts of Gallas. And the curses of saints and sharifs were considered, in Muhammadan countries, to be the most potent of all.[16]

Did the anathemas work? Certainly they did to a limited extent, because if they had not been believed in, and found purposeful, they would not have been used for more than a thousand years. The dozens just referred to are proof enough. Isn't it because of those same anathemas that the books in which they were written have survived? If anathemas failed, in the long run, it was often not because the books left the monastery, but because the monastery was destroyed or dissolved, leaving the books. The only true test of the anathema's utility is beyond our capability: to know how many books no longer exist which once wore their protection.

Why did anathemas go out of fashion? There are several possibilities. The growth of printing finally made the production of books so economical that a single volume ceased to represent an enormous expense calling for heavenly protection. Then too, perhaps the writer—and the reader—in later centuries lost typically medieval close association with religion, an association that had permeated so much of medieval everyday lives. And the anathema lost its ability to threaten. Those who lived after the Middle Ages looked back at the past and saw much of it, including anathemas, as quaint and even amusing. It became fashionable for authors and poets to express their cleverness or sense of whimsy by creating amusing anathemas; and even as late as the 19th century, anathemas were being written inside the covers of textbooks by children who knew nothing of the fine tradition of cursing, and whose only redeeming social merit was that they were to become our great-grandparents.

Even the anathemas that had been written in the time of their greatness are now seldom found. It is ironic that many of the books they were written to protect have survived while the anathemas were lost: the covers within which they were written, or the first or last pages on which they were penned, were the first to succumb either to deterioration, misuse, or the simple fact that they were ripped away by the thief to mask the theft.[53]

More anathemas were destroyed not by evil-doers, but by those with the best of intentions. In the 15th and 16th centuries many monastic books—original or duplicate copies sold by monasteries, or the former property of monasteries in England closed in the Reformation—came on the market legitimately, and their anathemas were therefore erased. Similarly, many 12th- and 13th-century monastic books were, at the end of the Middle Ages, given to colleges for their libraries—and the anathemas removed.[46]

Gone forever are the bulk of anathemas whose examples, on previous pages, probably represent only a tiny percentage. No longer does one expect to open a book and find, ready to pounce upon one's conscience from across the years or centuries, the likes of the following clutch of curses:

From the 8th century:

> *Liber Sancti*
> *Petri Gandensis ecclesie.*
> *Servanti benedictio,*
> *tollenti maledictio.*
> *Qui tulerit folium vel curtaverit,*
> *anathema sit.*

The book of Saint Peter at the church at Ghent. A blessing upon the one who keeps it safe, a curse upon the one who removes it. May whoever takes or cuts a page of it be accursed.

From the scriptorium of the Monastery of St. Pierre, in Ghent[50]

From the 8th or 9th centuries:

Si quis illum auferre tentaverit, judicium cum Deo et Sancto Medardo sibi habere non dubitet.

If anyone tries to carry this book away, may he not doubt that he will be judged in the sight of God and Saint Medardus.

From a manuscript of Cassiodorus's works on history, produced in the Monastery of Monte Cassino[15, 101]

* * *

Anathematizentur

> May they be accursed
>> From the scriptorium of Mayence. Rome,
>> Vatican Library, Pal. Lat. 577, folio 69 recto,
>> The Canons of Dionysius Exiguus[50]

From the 9th century:

Liber evangeliorum oblatus ad altare S. Stephani ex voto Agobardi episcopi. sit utenti gratia, largitori venia, fraudanti anathema.

The book of gospels presented at the altar of Saint Stephan in accordance with the vow of the bishop Agobardus. May grace be to the reader, indulgence to the benefactor, and a curse upon its thief.

>> Written about 825[101]

* * *

Nemo me credat omnino furatum,
Sed feliciter hactenus fuisse reservatum.
Non dubitet autem iram dei periculosius incurrere,
Si quis me praesumat a sancti Galli finibus spoliando auferre.

May no one believe that ever have I been taken,
But that happily this place never have I forsaken.
Yet may no one doubt that the wrath of God upon him will fall
If he essays to take me from the confines of St. Gall.

>> From the scriptorium of the
>> Monastery of St. Gall in 880[101]

* * *

Hic est liber Sancti Benedicti abbatis . . . coenobii; si quis eum aliquo ingenio non redditurus abstraxerit, cum Juda proditore, Anna et Caipha atque Pilato damnationem accipiat! amen.

This is the book of Saint Benedictus the abbot . . . at the monastery; if anyone by any means takes this book away without intending to return it, may he suffer eternal damnation with Judas the betrayer, with Annas and Caiphas and Pilate. Amen.[15]

From the 10th century:

Hic est liber S. Eripii ex Riopullensi monasterio. Si quis eum furaverit vel folias exinde abstraxerit anathema sit.

This is the book of Saint Eripius from the monastery at Ripoll. If anyone steals this book or takes a leaf from it, may he be accursed.

From Spain[101]

From the 11th century:

Hunc quicumque librum Aldhelmo depresseris almo,
Damnatus semper maneas cum sorte malorum.
Sit pietate Dei sine, qui vel portet ab isto
Coenobio librum Aldhelmi hunc vel vendere temptet.
Qui legis inscriptos versus, rogitare memento
Christum ac: In requie semper, dic, vivat Adhelwerd,
Qui dedit hunc thomum Aldhelmo, pro quo sibi Christus
Munera larga ferat, largitor crimina laxans.

Whoever steals this book from devoted Aldhelmus, may he always remain damned with the lot of the wicked. May he be without the pity of God who carries this book of Aldhelmus from this monastery or who tries to sell it. O reader of these lines, remember to beseech Christ saying, "May Adhelwerd always live in peace, who has given this book to Aldhelmus in return for which may Christ bear him bounteous gifts and pardon his sins.

From the scriptorium of Malmesbury Cloister, now Cambridge Cambridge, Corpus Christi Ms. 23[101]

From the 12th century:

Liber S. Marie sanctique Liborii in Patherburnen. tollenti maledictio servanti benedictio. Si quis abstulerit vel curtaverit folium anathema sit.

The book of Saint Marie and Saint Liborius in Patherburnen. A curse upon the one who takes this book, a blessing upon the one who keeps it safe. If anyone removes or cuts a page, may he be accursed.

From the year 1178[101]

*   *   *

Marcus glosatus quem dedit Lambinus de Brugis ecclesie sante Marie Ursicampi. Si quis abstulerit vel alienaverit quoque modo: anathema sit. Amen.

This is the Gospel of St. Mark which Lambinus of Bruges gave to the Church of St. Marie of Ourscamp. May he who takes it away or indeed loses it in any way be anathema.

From the last page of the Gospel written in the Cistercian Abbey of Ourscamp in the neighborhood of Compiegne (Oise)[53]

* * *

Si quis abstulerit vel curtaverit folium, anathema sit. Ricberti cura.

If anyone removes or cuts a page of this book, may he be accursed. The concern of Ricbertus.[101]

From the 13th century:

*Qui librum istum furatur,
a domino maledicatur.*

May he who steals this book
be cursed by the Lord.[101]

From the 14th century:

Qui nituntur eum auferre de fraternitate, descendant in infernum viventes cum Dathan et Abyron.

May those who endeavor to remove this book from the brotherhood, while still living descend into Hell with Dathan and Abiron.
                                                                From the year 1394[101]

From the 15th century:

*Qui che live emblera
A gibet de Paris pendu sera,
Et, si n'est pendu, il noiera,
Et, si ne noie, il ardera,*

> Et, si n'aert pitte fin fera.
> [A corrected reading of the last line:
> Et, si n'art, pire fin fera.]

Whoever steals this book
Will hang on a gallows in Paris,
And, if he isn't hung, he'll drown,
And, if he doesn't drown, he'll roast,
And, if he doesn't roast, a worse end will befall him.
>> *From a manuscript in the collection of*
>> *Jean d'Orleans, comte d'-Angouleme*[95]

* * *

No mon this book he take away,
    Ny kutt owte noo leef, y say for why;
For hyt ys sacrelege, sirus, y yow say,
    [He] beth acursed in the dede truly; . . .
>> *At the end of a manuscript composed*
>> *by blind and deaf John Awdelay, at the*
>> *monastery of Haughmond, 1426.*[14]

From the 16th century:

> My master's name above you se,
> Take heede therefore you steale not mee;
> For if you doe, without delay
> Your necke . . . for me shall pay.
> Looke doune below and you shal see
> The picture of the gallowstree;

Take heede therefore of thys in time,
Lest on this tree you highly clime.⁹⁵

*   *   *

Thomas Hyllbrond owe this book,
Whosoever will yt tooke,
Whoso stellyt shall be hangyd,
By ayre, by water, or by lande.
With a hempen bande.
God is where he was.
A° Vi. R. Edwardi vi.
*From a Sarum manuscript*⁹⁵

<u>*From the 17th century:*</u>

Who lets this book be lost,
Or doth embesell yt,
God's curse will to his cost,
Give him plagues in hell fytt.
*In the church register of
Sowe, Warwickshire, 1623*⁹⁵

<u>*And date unspecified:*</u>

Hic est liber S. Maximini, quem Hato armarius Deo et S. M. scribere fecit, tali tenore ut si quis eum ab oc loco non redditurus abstraxerit, cum diabolo damnationem accipiat. Amen. Fiat.

This is the book of Saint Maximinus which Hato, the librarian, commissioned to be written for God and Saint Maximinus at such expense that if anyone removes it from this place without intending to return it, may he be damned along with the devil. Amen. So be it.[101]

* * *

Offendit Christum, / qui librum subtrahit istum.

He offends Christ / who removes this book.[101]

* * *

Expl.(icit) tractatus ab Alberto Col. compositus de plantacionibus arborum. Ne fiat raptus liber plantantibus aptus, Observetur ne cui nequam tribuetur (sic).

This treatise on the planting of trees written by Albertus Col. for planters is finished. That this book may not be stolen, may it be guarded and may it not be given up to any worthless person.[101]

* * *

This blessed book belongs to the church of the monastery of Sinai, and whosoever takes it away or tears a leaf from it, may the Virgin be a foe to him, and may his fate be one with the fate of Judas Iscariot.

Arabic inscription on the fly-leaf of a Syriac manuscript in the Public Library, Leningrad[95]

* * *

Who folds a leafe downe
    ye divel toaste browne,
Who makes marke or blotte
    ye divel roaste hot,
Who stealeth thisse boke
    ye divel shall cooke.[95]

* * *

Qui te furetur,
cum Juda dampnificetur.

May he who steals you
be damned along with Judas.[101]

* * *

Thys boke ys sancht audatys;
he yt stelys this boke shall be haulynht by ye neck.
From a late Manuale.
London, British Museum
Ms. 30,506, leaf 170[101]

That the anathemas died, we can hold only ourselves to blame, because we have lost ability to fear them. This was brought home to me, both figuratively *and* literally, when a large envelope of reference material for this book arrived recently at my doorstep. The material had been gathered for me by Prof. Harvey who, because he labors in the Department of Classics at the University of Exeter, England, and

> PLEASE DO NOT BEND
> If anyone shall bend this, let him lie under perpetual malediction. Fiat fiat fiat. Amen. FART

Plate 27: HER MAJESTY'S POSTAL CURSE. We are to blame for the disappearance of the book curse: if one doesn't fear it, it no longer holds any validity. Prof. H. David Harvey employed a book curse, slightly altered, to protect an envelope of reference material on its journey through the British Postal System. The envelope arrived damaged. Not only had the curse not protected it, but an anonymous governmental hand had added a brief comment in one word, clearly indicating a reaction other than fear. Sad, indeed, to see so ancient an aspect of literary history die, and in no less ancient a land than England. But what other land can boast a governmental branch that not only appears medieval in operation, but is staffed by civil servants still fluent in 13th-century Anglo-Saxon?

is an expert in matters of Greek antiquity, is a friend whom I can affectionately say was born 2,000 years *behind* his time. Concerned for the safety of the material he was sending me, he had carefully inscribed on the face of the envelope (Plate 27)

> PLEASE DO NOT BEND
> If anyone shall bend this, let him lie under perpetual malediction. Fiat fiat fiat. Amen.

At some point on its way through Her Majesty's Postal System someone read the anathema and was moved to action. Compelled to respond to this ancient literary genre in equally archaic manner, he took pen in hand and countered in precise Anglo-Saxon, in usage familiar as far back, at least, as the 13th century:[62, 66, 102]

FART

and bent the envelope.

The heyday of the anathema is now half a thousand years behind us. No longer does the handling of a book invoke the wonders of disembowelment and damnation. Gone are the rack, the gallows, even the killer pigs of the Rhine. Open a book today and you realize how an eloquently deep past has become a shallow present. Where once echoed the fury of God now lies an insipid whimper:

> A fine of 5¢ per day will be charged . . .

APPENDIX
A CONFUSION OF BOOKS

Bring with thee the books, especially the parchments.
St. Paul to Timothy, 2 *Eph.* iv.13[59]

* * *

It is finished—let it finish!
Let the scribe go out to play.[17]

Explicit—Expliceat!
Ludere scriptor eat.
Scribe's final line in a
medieval manuscript.

As precious and as rare as books were, a religious life demanded that many be on hand. Because the same book often had different titles, and because differing arrangements of contents led to different titles, it can be confusing to understand what is specifically referred to. Following are some titles that would have been most common and in greatest demand at various times during the Middle Ages and shortly thereafter. All are service, instruction, or record books.* Not included are the works of Classical and medieval authors, teachers, and philosophers, although copies of their works were considered vital acquisitions. This list gives a brief idea of how much work the medieval scribe could find—given the time—and why he was so necessary a part of medieval life.[30, 33, 35, 45, 51, 57, 70, 89, 104, 107]

ACCENTUARIUS	A guide to the pronunciation of the penultima. Later a part of the BREVIARY.
AGENDA	See MANUAL.
ANTIPHONARIUM ANTIPHONARY ANTIPHONER	From *Antiphon*, a sentence recited before and after each psalm: a liturgical book for the choir's use, containing the antiphons and antiphonal chants which were sung at the Canonical Hours and at Mass, as well as the Invitatories, Hymns, Responds, Versicals, Collects and Capitula. Today the name refers only to those portions of the BREVIARY that are sung. The book was usually massive in page size so that a single copy, placed before the choir, could be read by all. Also called, in Rome, a CANTATORIUM. See also COUCHER.
APOSTOLUS	See LECTIONARY.
BAPTISTERIUM	Probably the earliest form of MANUALE, notable for its inclusion of material on the Rite of Baptism.

---

*For a clear and interesting account of the origin and meaning of the multitude of prayers, forms of service, rituals, etc., of the Catholic and Anglican churches which resulted in the production of these books, see Henry Barclay Swete, *Church Services and Service-Books Before the Reformation* (London and New York, 1905); and Christopher Wordsworth and Henry Littlehales, *The Old Service-Books of the English Church* (London, 1904).

BENEDICTIONAL	A book containing the forms of episcopal benedictions or blessings; specifically including the consecration of an abbot.
BIBLE BIBLIA BIBLIOTHECA	A gathering of the Old and New Testaments. Because of its size, it often consisted of more than one volume. The name is derived from the fact that in earliest times papyrus was exported to Mediterranean centers through the port of Byblos. *Biblos,* in Greek, meant "book" as well as "papyrus," and the most important of all books came to be called by that name.
BOOK OF COMMON PRAYER	The successor to all service books, in the Anglican Church, as of June 9, 1549. Almost invariably, each section of the book represented an earlier service book. See BREVIARY.
BOOK OF HOURS	A book designed for the laity, and small in size so that it could be carried to and from services. Its contents included the Calendar of Saints, four Gospel lessons, the order of service for each Canonical Hour, a Litany, Penitential Psalms, and the Office for the Dead. It was not uncommon for the owner of this volume to insert or pay a scribe to insert additional prayers that might be especially helpful, depending on the owner's needs or afflictions. See also PRIMER.
BREVARIUM BREVIARY	The equivalent of the BOOK OF COMMON PRAYER with the Proper Lessons, but lacking the Occasional Offices and the Communion Service. First known as a single volume in 1099, the Roman BREVIARY had earlier consisted of four divisions—PARS HIEMALIS, PARS VERNA, PARS ESTIVA, and PARS AUTUMNALIS—the

first and third of which, after about 1494, replaced the PORTIFORIA. The BREVIARY consisted of a Calendar of Saints, a PSALTER with VERSICALS and responses for each of the weekday Hours, and sometimes also the Small Offices. The BREVIARY was compiled for use in church and for priests' private recitations. See also PORTAS and TOTUM (a complete BREVIARY). In England the BREVIARY was called a PORTIFORIUM, probably for the simple reason that it was portable. After the PRIMER and PSALTER, it was the book most likely owned by lay people.

CALENDAR	See KALENDAR.
CANONS	The rules or laws or commandments of the Church. The oldest part of the Roman Mass. Canon, in Greek *kanon*, originally meant a "rod," and later any rule promoted by a rod or force.
CANON MISSAE	The CANON of the Mass lettered on rolls.
CANTATORIUM	See ANTIPHONARY.
CAPITULARY CAPITULUM	The collection of ordinances drawn up by the kings of the Franks, notably Charlemagne.
CARTULARY CHARTULARY	The place where all the papers or records of a monastery were kept, or the book into which they have been copied. From the Latin *cartularium* and *chartularium*.[64] See also LEGER and LEDGER.
CHRONICLES	Monasteries invariably kept continuing records of their activities, and added to the pages whenever possible was

information about the outside world learned from passersby and from monks returning from pilgrimages and errands. Because monks were sometimes called upon to help with secular paperwork outside the monastery, the details of these matters were sometimes added. Larger monasteries, given sufficient staff and inclination, had monks who devoted themselves to writing out the histories of their countries from the beginning of time to the then-present day.[9] While the records of the monastery were important to its inhabitants (often being the deciding factor when ancient land rights were questioned), a good portion of what we know of medieval Western history is the result of accumulated CHRONICLE notations made in idle curiosity; such CHRONICLES are in many cases the only surviving documents of their time.

COLLATIONUM LIBER	Book for Lenten readings.
COLLECTARIUM	Shorter lessons with Collects or short prayers. See also COLLECTARIUS.
COLLECTARIUS	This may be another name for COLLECTARIUM. But I have seen mention of it only once, and then referred to as an extremely rare liturgical volume designed especially for a bishop's use, and so I include it separately. The contents of one produced in about 1153 for the bishop of Constance Cathedral included the complete TEMPORAL from Christmas Eve to the fourth Sunday of Advent, the SANCTORALE, Common Prayers and benedictions for daily rounds, church dedication and anniversary, the bishop's birthday, on the occasions of em-

barking on a journey and traveling by sea, and in the events of war and of plague, etc.[85]

COLLECT-BOOK	Correctly COLLECT AND CHAPTER-BOOK. See COLLECTARIUM and COLLECTARIUS.
COMES	See LECTIONARY.
COMMUNE DE TEMPORE	See PSALTER.
COSTUMARY CONSUETUDINARIUS CONSUETUDINARY	The book of customs (the ritual and ceremonial usages) of a monastic establishment or order. Not to be interchangeable with RULE.
COPY BOOK	See MODEL BOOK.
COUCHER COWCHER	See LEGER.
DIRECTORIUM	See ORDINALE.
DIRGE-BOOK	The Office for the Dead.
DIURNALE	BOOK OF HOURS of the Day, covered by the BREVIARY. In use until 1549.
ENCHIRIDION	See FLORILEGIUM.
EPISTOLARIA EPISTOLARIUM EPISTOLARY	See LECTIONARY.
EVANGELIARIA EVANGELIARIUM EVANGELISTARIUM	The GOSPELS. See LECTIONARY.

EXULTET ROLL	A roll containing a portion of the Easter Even Services.	
FLORILEGIUM	The title given to an ENCHIRIDION or personal notebook. St. Augustine defined it as "a book not for the shelf or the cupboard, but for the hands." In it the monk jotted down anything and everything that attracted his interest, making it a scrapbook of useful or simply curious information. If he were an author, the FLORILEGIUM might be the means of collecting information to be later reworked and reorganized as a formal presentation. But it was not uncommon for an author simply to recopy the FLORILEGIUM neatly, without any changes, and distribute it. This in itself was considered a worthwhile literary contribution. The word in Latin means a gathering of flowers; for that is all it was—a gathering, without organization or particular reason—of whatever appealed to the monk.[8]* Any original FLORILEGIUM is usually sloppily written, with lines of text and margins uneven. It is thus a joy to the eye of the modern calligrapher who feels daunted by the grace and uniformity of almost any other medieval manuscript; it is proof that most medieval scribes were unable to write neatly without first ruling guidelines. Their basic inability is immediately evident because the FLORILEGIUM was the only manuscript in which they wrote without first preparing guidelines.	
GOSPELS	The first four books of the New Testament, comprising the teachings of Christ and the Apostles.	

*Thus the term *anthology*, from the Greek *anthos* (flower) and *lego* (gather); an *anthologia* (flower-gathering), or collection of extracts from one or many sources.[30]

GRADALE GRADUAL GRAIL GRAYLE	The GRADUALS or Psalms which are sung between the Epistle and the GOSPEL; quite often also included the music for the liturgy of the Mass and other parts of the service to be sung. It later included the TROPER. See also MISSAL and TROPER.	
HOMILARIES	A collection of books of sermons used by clergymen who were unable to, or chose not to, write their own.	
HOMILIARIUS	See LEGENDA.	
HORAE	See BOOK OF HOURS	
HYMNARIUM HYMNARY	Collection of Office Hymns which were contained, after the 11th century, in the BREVIARY or ANTIPHONARY.	
JOURNAL	See DIURNALE.	
KALENDAR	The KALENDAR, or main list of fixed festivals listed chronologically for the given year, never appeared as a volume in itself, but was part of the BREVIARY. I list it here separately because, since KALENDARS were of such importance, their pages were often decorated, and modern publishers reproducing medieval art frequently illustrate their books with KALENDARS and give the impression that they may have been books in themselves. KALENDARS are beneficial to paleographers because they list saints and ceremonies of interest only in the locale for which the KALENDAR was prepared, so that a BREVIARY's KALENDAR often contains the clues as to where it originated (or was destined). And KALENDARS are valuable to calligraphers looking for authentic letter shapes:	

the letter *k* is rarely used in manuscript texts but can always be found in the KALENDAR.

LECTIONARIUM LECTIONARY	The parts of the Epistles and GOSPELS to be read aloud on specific days of the Church year. Also called an EPISTOLARY, EPISTOLARIUM, APOSTOLUS and COMES.
LEGENDA LEGENDARIUS	Sermons, hagiographies (lives of the saints), lessons from the BIBLE (SERMOLOGUS), and all the passages read at Matins, to be used at divine services. The LEGENDA originally consisted of the SERMOLOGUS and HOMILIARIUS (patristic sermons and expositions), PASSIONARIUS (sufferings of the Martyrs) and LEGENDARIUS (Acts of the Saints). It later became part of the MISSAL. See MISSAL.
LEGER	A general term meaning any Service book (most likely an ANTIPHONER, LEGENDER, BREVIARY, or MISSAL) so large that it was inconvenient to hold upright or to store on end. It was therefore kept lying down and infrequently or never moved. From the French "to lie down" and therefore understandably also called a COUCHER or COWCHER; also, from the Latin "book lying down," called a LIBER DORMIENS.
LEDGER	A book of accounts and/or records, probably so large that its name originated in LEGER. See LEGER and CARTULARY.
LIBER DORMIENS	See LEGER.

LIBER MATUTINALIS	A counterpart to the DIURNALE. See DIURNALE.	
LIBER PONTIFICALIS	See PONTIFICAL.	
LIBRA SACRAMENTORUM	See SACRAMENTARY.	
LIBRI POENITENTIALES	See POENITENTIAL.	
LITANIES	See PROCESSIONAL.	

MANUAL
MANUALE
MANUELL

A small book of instruction (probably at first called a BAPTISTERIUM) comprising the Occasional Services (baptism, marriage and burial, Office for the Dead, and LITANY). Those services which were to be performed only by a bishop were written in the PONTIFICALE. The MANUAL was also called an AGENDA, a MANUALE, MANUELL, a PASTORALE, a SACRAMENTALE, SACRAMENTARIUM and, on the continent of Europe, a RITUALE.

MARTILOGE
MARTYROLOGY
MARTYROLOGIUM

A more-complete KALENDAR. See KALENDAR.

MISSAL
MISSALE
MISSALE PLENARIUM
MISSALE SPECIALE

For the *missa* (thus *mass*). A service book in which many different materials were gathered. In the 9th century it was occasionally called a MISSALE PLENARIUM. From the 7th century onward it was known as a SACRAMENTARY and contained the COLLECTS, Secrets, Prefaces, CANONS, and Post-Communions. The GOSPELS, Lessons, Epistles, and sung portions of the Mass were housed in other volumes, and all the volumes together were known as a MISSALE PLENARIUM. When it became customary to put everything in one volume, the second word was eliminated. By gathering everything together the resultant volume was so large and expensive that some churches, particularly in Germany and Switzerland, used abridged versions containing only the text of Masses for Sundays and special feast days. This was called a MISSALE SPECIALE. At some point, the MISSAL included the PROCESSIONAL and LITANIES, the LECTIONARY, EVANGELISTARIUM, GRADALE and the TROPER.

MODEL BOOK

A manuscript owned by a scribe or the property of a scriptorium. Also known as a COPY BOOK. It contained alphabets in various scripts, brief passages of religious services, perhaps also decorative designs—anything a scribe might have to look up to refresh his memory. Scribes who owned their own MODEL BOOKS could become quite protective of them; borrowing one without permission could lead to physical violence, and there is one recorded case of the borrower being slain. The culprit was understandably, as any calligrapher today would appreciate, pardoned. See also PATTERN BOOK.

ORDINAL
ORDINALE
ORDINARIUM
ORDINIS

Rules for finding the correct sequence for different parts of the service, which could change due to movable feasts. Known as a PICA or PICA DE SARUM, and as a PIE because of its "pied" appearance due to the initial letters all being written in red. The ORDINAL later became part of the MISSAL.

PARS HIEMALIS PARS VERNA PARS ESTIVA PARS AUTUMNALIS	Divisions of the Roman BREVIARY when it was not produced as a single volume. See BREVIARY.	
PASSIONAL PASSIONARIUS	Accounts of the lives of the saints and martyrs. Rendered unnecessary by the 11th-century arrival of the BREVIARY. See also LEGENDA.	
PASTORAL PASTORALE	See MANUAL.	
PATTERN BOOK	Like a COPY BOOK or MODEL BOOK, but specifically containing partial and complete drawings and complex patterns which the scribe (or illuminator in later times) could refer to as needed. The designs and drawings in a PATTERN BOOK might be outlined with pin-holes, as a means of transferring the outlines to the page on which the artist was working. The PATTERN BOOK design was brushed with pounce, which would filter through the pin-holes and create a dotted pattern of powder on the working sheet. See MODEL BOOK.	
PENITENTIAL	See POENITENTIAL.	
PICA PICA DE SARUM PIE PYE	Also called a DIRECTORIUM. The PICA was at some late date included in the BREVIARY. See ORDINAL and BREVIARY.	
POCKET BREVIARY	See PORTAS and BREVIARY.	

APPENDIX 123

POENITENTIAL	A manual of disciplinary instructions; a collection of CANONS that set the exact penance for each sin specified. See CANON.	
PONTIFICAL PONTIFICALE	The ceremonies and offices performed specifically by a bishop, including the BENEDICTIONAL; i.e., to confirm, ordain, and consecrate churches and churchyards; bless everyone and everything dedicated to God's service, be it abbot, abbess, king, queen, vestment, or book; expel the penitents and reconcile them after their penance.	
PORTACE PORTAS PORTASSE PORTATILIA PORTEFORS PORTHOS PORTHORS PORTIFORIUM PORTOS PORTOUS PORTUISSE PORTUORIE	A BREVIARY written in such small script and on such thin vellum pages that it could be conveniently carried by a traveling cleric. It later came to mean any MANUAL of philosophy or some other subject. After about 1494 the PORTACE was divided into two volumes, the PARS HIEMALIS and PARS ESTIVA. See BREVIARY.	
PRICKSONG	A book of written descant or accompanying melody for a plain-song; or a book of organ music. So called because the music was "pricked", i.e., written, as opposed to sung by ear or from memory.	
PRIMARIUM PRIMER	A devotional BOOK OF HOURS that was part of the PSALTER until the 13th century; the standard lay pray-	

PRIMMER PRYMER	erbook and thus the one religious book most likely to be owned by an individual. The first record of its existence as a separate volume, known as a PRIMARIUM, occurs in 1294 and may refer to the Prime, or first of the Hours. In 1539 the bishop of Rochester suggested that the title was so-called because PRIMMERS were "the first books in which the young were instructed." The collection of the Hours of the Virgin, the Office for the Dead, and the LITANY later had its name, PRIMARIUM, Anglicized to PRIMMER, PRYMER or PRIMER. Since it was a personal rather than Service book, it was decorated at the owner's whim and wealth.	
PROCESSIONAL PROCESSIONALE	The services including the LITANIES (from the Greek for supplication) involved in a procession or march of church dignitaries around the building or to or from the altar. Royal decree in England abolished processions in 1547: the king* was annoyed by the cacophony that arose among those in the procession who objected to their assigned locations in the procession which indicated, like seating above and below the salt at table, their importance.	
PROPRIUM SANCTORUM	See SANCTORALE.	
PRYMER	See PRIMER.	
PSALTER	A collection of Psalms, divided into eight sections (one	

*Probably not Henry VIII, as he spent the first 28 days of 1547 unpleasantly but successfully dying. More likely his son Edward VI who, as a nine-year-old in the procession, might easily have been displeased (if not frightened) by the malcontents.

for each day plus Vespers), designed to be read through every week. Generally included were a KALENDAR, the Canticles, the Athanasian Creed and LITANY. It was used by monks and by laymen, the most important and most common devotional book in the early Middle Ages. The nonliturgical PSALTER contained Psalms without intervening material. The liturgical PSALTER was a Service book with ANTIPHONS, etc., following certain Psalms. By the 13th century the Office for the Dead became included in the PSALTER. Also called a COMMUNE DE TEMPORE.

PYE-BOOK — See ORDINAL.

QUIRES
QUATERNIONES — Small copy-books stitched but not bound. Not to be confused with COPY BOOK.

REGULA — See RULE.

RESPONSORARY
RESPONSORY — Perhaps another name for ANTIPHONALE and GRADUAL. A book of music for anthems in which a soloist and choir alternate responsively.

RITUALE — See MISSAL and MANUAL.

RULE — A statement of the purpose for the establishment of a monastic community, and a detailing of the responsibilities and requirements imposed upon each member of the community.

SACRAMENTAL
SACRAMENTARIUM — An early MISSAL without Epistles or GOSPELS, designed as a Service book for bishops. It was replaced by the

SACRAMENTARY	MISSAL in the later Middle Ages. See MISSAL and MANUAL.	
SANCTORAL SANCTORALE	That part of the MISSAL and BREVIARY relating to offices pertinent to saints' days. See MISSAL and BREVIARY.	
SARUM USE	A medieval modification, by the diocese of Salisbury in the 11th century, of the BOOK OF HOURS and MISSAL. By the end of the Middle Ages this version was the most common in use in England. "Sarum" is the name of the original Roman fort and settlement which became the diocese of Salisbury. See BOOK OF HOURS and MISSAL.	
SERMOLOGUS	See LEGENDA.	
SHRIFT-BOOK	See POENITENTIAL.	
STANDARDS	Perhaps a general term for music books so large as to be read by several persons at one time.	
TABULA	A paper rather than book, listing who was responsible for each facet of every service, week by week. It was read to all on Saturdays (after Prime) and posted. A TABULA was also a board smeared with green wax, on whose surface the information was scratched (the wax conveniently being smoothed over when the information was to be changed). Also called a WAX-BREDE or WEAX-BRED (wax-board?).	
TONARIUS TONALE	A collection of ANTIPHONS with tone endings. Not required by authority.	
TOTUM	See BREVIARY.	

TROPER	A book of musical interpolations or Tropes (verses sung with the Introit) and Sequences (hymns sung after the GRADUAL). The TROPER was discontinued when Pope Pius V (1566-1572) revised the MISSAL, and became part of the latter and of the GRAIL. See MISSAL and GRAIL.
VENITARE	A music book of the Invitatories at the beginning of Mattins.
VERSICULARE VERSICLE	A collection of verses or versicles relating to the BIBLE.
VULGATE BIBLE	Translation by St. Jerome of the BIBLE into Latin.
WAX-BREDE WEAX-BRED	See TABULA.

SOURCES

> Styll am I besy bokes assemblynge,
> For to have plenty it is a pleasant thynge
> In my conceyt, and to have them ay in honde;
> But what they mene I do nat understone.
>
> Pynson's *Ship of Fools*,
> edit. 1509[22]

1. Alexander, David, and Pat Alexander, eds. *Eerdmans' Handbook to the Bible.* Grand Rapids, Mich., 1973.
2. Alexander, J.J.G. *Italian Renaissance Illumination.* London, 1977.
   _____. *The Decorated Letter.* New York, 1978.
   _____. *Insular Manuscripts—6th to 9th Century. A Survey of Manuscripts Illuminated in the British Isles,* Vol. I. London, 1978.
   _____. "Scribes as Artists: The Arabesque Initial in Twelfth Century English Manuscripts." In M. B. Parks and Andrew G. Watson, *Medieval Scribes, Manuscripts and Libraries, Essays Presented to N. R. Ker.* London, 1978.
   Alexander, J.J.G., and A. C. DeLaMere. *The Italian Manuscripts in the Library of Major J. R. Abbey.* London, 1969.
3. Anonymous. *Two References to the English Book-Trade, Circa 1525.* In *Bibliographica,* Part II. London, n.d.
4. Ascherl, Joseph P. "Monks and Book Publishing—Eighth Century." In *The Church Bulletin.* Floral Park, N.Y., n.d.

5. Barlow, Frank, Kathleen M. Dexter, Audrey M. Erskine, and L. J. Lloyd. *Leofric of Exeter—Essays in Commemoration of the Foundation of Exeter Cathedral Library in A.D. 1072.* Exeter, 1972.
6. Barrett, Dom Michael. *A Calendar of Scottish Saints.* Fort Augustus, 1905(?).
7. Birchenough, Edwyn. "The Prymer in English." In *The Library, Transactions of the Bibliographical Society,* 2nd Ser., Vol. 18. Republished 4th Ser., Vol. 18. London, 1938.
8. Brearley, Denis. "The Collectaneum of Sedulius Scottus and Ninth-Century Hiberno-Latin Florilegia." Paper presented at the Conference on Latin Texts and Manuscripts of the British Isles, 550–1066, Glendon College, York University, Toronto. April 1979.
9. British Museum. *A Catalogue of the Lansdowne Manuscripts in The British Museum.* London, 1819.
   _____. *A Guide to the Manuscripts, Autographs, Charters, Seals, Illuminations and Bindings Exhibited in The Department of Manuscripts and in the Granville Library.* London, 1899.
10. Buhler, Curt F., ed. *Treasures from the Pierpont Morgan Library—Fiftieth Anniversary Exhibition, 1957.* New York, 1957.
    _____. *The Fifteenth-Century Book—The Scribes—The Printers—The Decorators.* Philadelphia, 1960.
    _____. "Remarks on the Printing of the Augsburg Edition (c. 1474) of Bishop Salomon's Glossae." In Hellmut Lehmann-Haupt, ed., *Homage to a Bookman—Essays on Manuscripts, Books, and Printing Written for Hans P. Kraus on his 60th Birthday Oct. 12, 1967.* Berlin, 1967.
    _____. *Early Books and Manuscripts—Forty Years of Research,* 1973. (City not indicated)
11. Butler, Dom Cuthbert. *St. Benedict's Rule for Monasteries.* Translated by Leonard J. Doyle. St. Louis, 1935. Reprint Collegeville, Minn., 1948.
12. Clark, Anne. *Beasts and Bawdy.* New York, 1975.
13. Clark, John Willis. *The Care of Books—An Essay on the Development of Libraries and their Fittings, from the Earliest Times to the End of the Eighteenth Century.* Cambridge, 1901.
    _____. *Libraries in the Medieval and Renaissance Periods.* 1894. Reprint Chicago, 1968.
14. Coulton, G. G. *A Medieval Garner: Human Documents from the Four Centuries Preceding the Reformation.* London, 1910.
    _____. *Social Life in Britain from the Conquest to the Reformation.* London, 1917(?).
    _____. *Five Centuries of Religion.* London, 1929. Excerpted in *The History of Popular Culture,* edited by Norman F. Cantor and Michael S. Werthman. New York and London, 1968.

———. *The Medieval Scene—An Informal Introduction to the Middle Ages*. Cambridge, 1930.
———. *The Meaning of Medieval Moneys*. Historical Association Leaflet no. 95. London, 1934.
———. *Europe's Apprenticeship: A Survey of Medieval Latin with Examples*. London, 1940.
———. *Art and the Reformation*. Cambridge, 1953.
15. Cruwell, G. A. *Die Verfluchung des Bucherdiebes*. Vol. 4 in *Archiv fur Kulturgeschicthe*. 1906.
16. Crawley, Ernest. *Oath, Curse and Blessing—And Other Studies in Origins*, Vol. 40, *The Thinker's Library*. London, 1940.
17. Culpa, Mea; my notes regarding the source(s) for this material have been lost.
18. Cutts, Edward L. *Scenes and Characters in the Middle Ages*. London, 1972.
19. De Bury, Richard. *Philobiblon—Richard de Bury*. Translated by Thomas. Oxford, 1960.
———. *Philobiblon, by Richard de Bury*. Translated by Archer Taylor. Berkeley, 1948.
20. Derolez, Albert. *The Library of Raphael de Marcatellis, Abbot of St. Bavon's, Ghent 1437-1508*. Ghent, 1979.
21. De Roover, Florence Edler. "The Medieval Library." Chapter 18 in *The Medieval Library*, edited by James Westfall Thompson. New York, 1957.
22. Dibdin, Thomas Frognall. *The Bibliomania; or Book-Madness; Containing Some Account of the History, Symptoms, and Cure of this Fatal Disease. Etc*. London, 1809.
23. Donaldson, Gerald. *Books—Their History, Art, Power, Glory, Infamy and Suffering According to Their Creators, Friends and Enemies*. New York, 1981.
24. Duncan, Judith Anne. *A Small Book of Book Curses*. Minneapolis, 1977.
25. Dutton, Paul, Pontifical Institute of Mediaeval Studies, Toronto, personal communication.
26. Edler, Florence. "The Monastic Scriptorium." *Thought*, 6, no. 2 (September 1931).
27. *Encyclopedia Britannica*. Chicago and London, 1960.
28. Fitzgerald, Wilma L., Pontifical Institute of Mediaeval Studies, Toronto, personal communication.
29. Forsyth, William. "History of Ancient Manuscripts." Lecture delivered in the Hall of the Inner Temple. London, 1872.
30. Funk, Wilfred. *Word Origins and Their Romantic Stories*. New York, 1978.
31. Ganz, David, University of North Carolina, Chapel Hill, translation courtesy of.
32. Gardthausen, V. *Griechische Palaeographie*. Leipzig, 1913.

33. Gasquet, Francis Aidan. *The Old English Bible and Other Essays.* London, 1897.
    ———. *English Monastic Life.* London, 1904.
    ———. *The Greater Abbeys of England.* London, 1908.
    ———. *Monastic Life in the Middle Ages.* London, 1922.
34. Gibson, Katharine. *The Goldsmith of Florence: A Book of Great Craftsmen.* New York, 1929.
35. Glaister, Geoffrey Ashall. *Glaister's Glossary of the Book-Terms Used in Papermaking, Printing, Bookbinding and Publishing, with Notes on Illuminated Manuscripts and Private Presses.* 2nd ed. Berkeley and Los Angeles, 1980.
36. Goldschmidt, E. P. *Medieval Texts and Their First Appearance in Print.* Supplement to the *Bibliographical Society Transactions* 16. Oxford, 1943. Reprint Germany, 1965.
37. Hartley, Dorothy. *Lost Country Life.* New York, 1979.
38. Harvey, F. David, University of Exeter, translation courtesy of, and personal communication.
39. Haskins, Charles Homer. *The Rise of the Universities.* Ithaca, 1923. 11th printing, 1969.
    ———. *The Renaissance of the Twelfth Century.* London, 1927.
40. Hindman, Sandra, and James Douglas Farquhar. *Pen to Press: Illustrated Manuscripts and Printed Books in the First Century of Printing.* Maryland, 1977.
41. Ivy, G. S. "The Bibliography of the Manuscript-Book." In *The English Library Before 1700*, edited by Francis Wormald and C. E. Wright. London, 1958.
42. Jackson, Donald. *The Story of Writing.* New York, 1981.
43. Jackson, Holbrook. *The Anatomy of Bibliomania.* New York, n.d.
44. Johnston, Harold W. *Latin Manuscripts: An Elementary Introduction to the Use of Critical Editions for High School and College Classes.* The Inter-Collegiate Latin Series. Chicago, 1897.
45. Kauffmann, C. M. *Romanesque Manuscripts 1066–1190: A Survey of Manuscripts Illuminated in the British Isles,* vol. 3. London, 1975.
46. Ker, N. R. "The Migration of Manuscripts from the English Medieval Libraries." In *The Library, Transactions of the Bibliographical Society,* 4th Ser., Vol. 23. London, 1942.
47. Kibre, Pearl. *Scholarly Privileges in the Middle Ages: The Rights, Privileges, and Immunities, of Scholars and Universities at Bologna, Padua, Paris & Oxford.* Medieval Academy of America Publication no. 72. Cambridge, Mass., 1962.

48. Lemprière, J. *Bibliotheca Classica; or, a Classical Dictionary, Containing a Full Account of all the Proper Names Mentioned in Antient Authors,* . . . Dublin, 1793.
49. Lewis, Naphtali. *Papyrus in Classical Antiquity.* Oxford, 1974.
50. Lindsay, W. M. *Early Irish Minuscule Script.* St. Andrew's University Publications no. 6. Oxford, 1910.

    _____. *Early Welsh Script.* St. Andrew's University Publications no. 10. Oxford, 1912.

    _____. *Palaeographia Latina,* Parts 1 through 6. St. Andrew's University Publications. Oxford and London, 1922-29.

    Lindsay, W. M., and P. Lehmann. "The (Early) Mayence Scriptorium." In *Palaeographia Latina,* Part 4. St. Andrew's University Publications no. 20. London, 1925.
51. Madan, Falconer. *Books in Manuscript: A Short Introduction to Their Study and Use.* London, 1920.

    _____. *Oxford—Outside the Guide-Books.* Oxford, 1923.

    _____. "Handwriting." In *Medieval England - A New Edition of Barnard's Companion to English History,* edited by H.W.C. Davis. Oxford, 1924.

    _____. *The Summary Catalogue of Western Manuscripts in the Bodleian Library,* vol. I. Oxford, 1966.
52. Maggs, H. Clifford, personal communication.
53. Maggs Brothers, Ltd. *The Art of Writing—2800 B.C. to 1930 A.D.—Illustrated in A Collection of Original Documents Written on Vellum, Paper, Papyrus, Silk, Linen, Bamboo, or Inscribed on Clay, Marble, Steatite, Jasper, Haematite Matrix of Emerald and Chalcedony—etc.* Catalogue 542. London, 1930.

    _____. *Charters of England, France, Germany, Italy, Scotland and Spain, from the 12th to the 17th Century.* London, 1982.
54. Maitland, S. R. *The Dark Ages; A Series of Essays, Intended to Illustrate the State of Religion and Literature in the Ninth, Tenth, Eleventh and Twelfth Centuries.* London, 1853. Reprinted in 2 vols., Port Washington, N.Y., 1969.
55. Martial (Marcus Valerius Martialis). *Martial—Selected Epigrams,* translated by Rolfe Humphries. Bloomington, Ind., 1963.
56. Mason, William A. *A History of the Art of Writing.* New York, 1920.
57. Maude, J. H. *The History of the Book of Common Prayer.* New York, 1904.

58. McKay, J. B., personal communication.
59. Merrill, George E. *The Story of the Manuscripts*. Boston, 1881.
60. Metzger, Bruce M. "When Did Scribes Begin to Use Writing Desks?" In *New Testament Tools and Studies*, vol. 8 of *Historical and Literary Studies, Pagan, Jewish, and Christian*. Grand Rapids, Mich., 1968.
61. Mitchell, Donald G. *English Lands Letters and Kings—From Celt to Tudor*. New York, 1889.
62. Onions, C. T., ed. *The Oxford Dictionary of English Etymology*. Oxford, 1966.
63. Orel, Harold, ed. *Irish History and Culture: Aspects of a People's Heritage*. Lawrence, Kan., 1976.
64. *Oxford English Dictionary*. Oxford, 1971.
65. Parassoglou, George M. "Some Thoughts on the Postures of the Ancient Greeks and Romans when Writing on Papyrus Rolls." In *Scrittura e Civilita . . .* , vol. 3. 1979.
66. Partridge, Eric. *A Dictionary of Slang and Unconventional English*. New York, 1970.
67. Pearson, Charles H. *The Early and Middle Ages of England*. 1861. Reprint Port Washington, N.Y., and London, 1971.
68. Petti, Anthony G. *English Literary Hands from Chaucer to Dryden*. Cambridge, Mass., 1977.
69. Pollard, Alfred W. *Early Illustrated Books—A History of the Decoration and Illustration of Books in the 15th and 16th Centuries*. London, 1893.
———. *An Essay on Colophons—With Specimens and Translations*. Chicago, 1905.
70. Posner, Raphael, and Israel Ta-Shema, eds. *The Hebrew Book: An Historical Survey*. Jerusalem, 1975.
71. Putnam, George Haven. *Books and Their Makers During the Middle Ages*, Vol. I. 1896-97. Reprint New York, 1962.
———. *Authors and Their Public in Ancient Times*. New York and London, 1923.
72. Radford, E., and M. A. Radford. *Encyclopaedia of Superstitions*. London and New York, 1948(?).
73. Rawlings, Gertrude Burford. *The Story of Books*. New York, 1904.
74. Richardson, Ernest Cushing. *Some Old Egyptian Librarians*. New York, 1911.
75. Robb, David M. *The Art of the Illuminated Manuscript*. South Brunswick, New York, and London, 1973.
76. Roberts, W., ed. *Book-Verse—An Anthology of Poems of Books and Bookmen from the Earliest Times to Recent Years*. London, 1896.

77. Robinson, Fred. "Varieties of Glossing in Latin Manuscripts from Anglo-Saxon England." Paper presented at The Conference on Latin Texts and Manuscripts of the British Isles, 550–1066, Glendon College, York University, Toronto. April 1979.
78. Roche, Aloysius. *A Bedside Book of Saints.* London, 1934.
 ———. *A Bedside Book of Irish Saints.* London, 1941.
 ———. *A Bedside Book of English Saints.* London, 1943.
79. Royal Ontario Museum of Archaeology. *Books of the Middle Ages.* 1950.
80. Savage, Ernest A. *Old English Libraries—The Making, Collection, and Use of Books During the Middle Ages.* London, 1911.
81. Schramm, Wilbur L. "The Cost of Books in Chaucer's Time." In *Modern Language Notes* 48, no. 3 (March 1933).
82. Semler, Mrs. George H., Jr., Pierpont Morgan Library, personal communication.
83. Skeat, T. C. "The Use of Dictation in Ancient Book Production." In *Proceedings of the British Academy.* London, 1956(?).
84. Smith, R.A.H., personal communication.
85. Sotheby & Co. *Bibliotheca Phillippica. New Series: Medieval Manuscripts. Part V—Catalogue of Manuscripts on Papyrus, Vellum and Paper, of the 13th Century B.C. to the 18th Century A.D. . . . November, 1969 . . .* London, 1969.
 ———. *Bibliotheca Phillippica—Medieval Manuscripts: New Series: Part VIII / Catalogue of Manuscripts on Vellum, Paper and Papyrus of the 4th to the 17th Century.* London, 1973.
 ———. *Catalogue of Valuable Printed Books and Manuscripts of the XVth to the XVIIIth Century.* London, 1974.
 ———. *Catalogue of Western Manuscripts and Miniatures . . . which will be sold by auction Tuesday, 8th December, 1981.* London, 1981.
 ———. *Catalogue of Twenty Western Illuminated Manuscripts from the Fifth to the Fifteenth Century, From the Library at Donaueschingen—the Property of His Serene Highness the Prince Furstenberg . . . Monday, 21st June 1982.* London, 1982.
86. Stone, J. M. *Studies from Court and Cloister—Being Essays, Historical and Literary, Dealing Mainly with Subjects Relating to the XVIth and XVIIth Centuries.* London, 1905.

87. Storms, Godfrid. *Anglo-Saxon Magic*. The Hague, 1948.
88. Swarzenski, Hanns. *Harvard College Library: Illuminated and Calligraphic Manuscripts—An Exhibition Held at the Fogg Art Museum and Houghton Library February 14–April 1, 1955.* Cambridge, Mass., 1955.
89. Swete, Henry Barclay. *Church Services and Service-Books Before the Reformation.* London and New York, 1905.
90. Tafel, S. "The Lyons Scriptorium." In *Palaeographia Latina*, Part 4, edited by W. M. Lindsay. St. Andrew's University Publications no. 20. London, 1925.
91. Talbot, C. H. "The Universities and the Medieval Library." In *The English Library Before 1700*, edited by Francis Wormald and C. E. Wright. London, 1958.
92. Taylor, Isaac. *History of the Transmission of Ancient Books to Modern Times; Together with the Process of Historical Proof, etc.* Liverpool, 1875.
93. Thompson, James Westfall. *The Literacy of the Laity in the Middle Ages.* University of California Publications in Education, vol. 9. Berkeley, 1939.
 ———. *The Medieval Library.* New York, 1957.
 ———. *Ancient Libraries.* Berkeley, CA., Reprint, Hamden, Conn., and London, 1962.
94. Thompson, Lawrence, ed. *The Development of the Book: A Guide to the First (Second, Third, Fourth) Exhibition in a Series Illustrating the Accumulated Heritage of the Modern Book, Princeton University Library.* 4 vols. Princeton, 1938 and 1939.
95. Thompson, Lawrence S. "Notes on Bibliokleptomania." *Bulletin of the New York Public Library* 48, no. 9 (1944).
 ———. "A Cursory Survey of Maledictions." *Bulletin of the New York Public Library*, February, 1952. Reprinted in *Bibliologia Comica or Humorous Aspects of the Caparisoning and Conservation of Books*, 1968.
96. Thorndike, Lynn. "Copyists' Final Jingles in Medieval Manuscripts." *Speculum* 12 (1937). Boston.
 ———. "More Copyists' Final Jingles." *Speculum* 31 (1956). Boston.
97. Tomkeieff, O. G. *Life in Norman England.* London and New York, 1966.
98. Trinity College Library, Cambridge. *Catalogue of Manuscripts.* N.d.

EXPLICIT

This book was written for the joy
I hold in things medieval,
And as a means of expediting
All the facts' retrieval,
On how my predecessors worked
And grumbled or found pleasure
In mundane endless copying
Of pages we now treasure.

To those who cannot write for spit
But think this book no task,
You just don't know the half of it
So I, to Heaven, ask:

Anathema! on anyone
Who takes so little care
That this, my latest work, should chance
To fall in disrepair.
And if you steal this copy, oh,
Invidious disloyalty;
Anathema! upon your soul—
I could have used the royalty.

Marc Drogin

99. Walker, C.B.F., Dept. of Western & Asiatic Antiquities, British Museum, London, personal communication.
100. Warner, Sir George F., and Julius Gilson. *British Museum Catalogue of Western Manuscripts in the Old Royal and King's Collections.* 4 vols. Oxford, 1921.
101. Wattenbach, Wilhelm. *Das Schriftwesen im Mittelalter.* Leipzig, 1896.
102. Weekley, Ernest. *An Etymological Dictionary of Modern English.* New York, 1967.
103. Weiss, Roberto. "The Private Collector and the Revival of Greek Learning." In *The English Library Before 1700,* edited by Francis Wormald and C. E. Wright. London, 1958.
104. Wenzel, Siegfried. *The Sin of Sloth: Acedia–In Medieval Thought and Literature.* Chapel Hill, N.C., n.d.
105. Williams, John. *Early Spanish Manuscript Illumination.* New York, 1977.
106. Williams, Thomas Webb. *Somerset Medieval Libraries.* Somerset Archaeological and Natural History Society, Northern Branch. Bristol, 1897.
107. Wordsworth, Christopher, and Henry Littlehales. *The Old Service-Books of the English Church.* London, 1904.
108. Wright, Thomas. *Essays on Subjects Connected with the Literature, Popular Superstitions and History of England in the Middle Ages.* 1846. Reprint New York, 1969.

> Let but the morn appear, I'll run
> To every bookstall in the town.
> *Catullus*[76]